W9-ANP-718

Hymns of the Eastern Church.

AMS PRESS
NEW YORK

HYMNS

OF

THE EASTERN CHURCH:

TRANSLATED,

WITH NOTES AND AN INTRODUCTION,

BY

THE REV. J. M. NEALE, D.D.,
Warden of Sackville College.

LONDON:

J. T. HAYES, 5, LYALL PLACE, EATON SQ.

1862.

Reprinted from the edition of 1862, London
First AMS EDITION published 1971
Manufactured in the United States of America

International Standard Book Number: 0-404-04666-5

Library of Congress Number: 77-131029

AMS PRESS INC.
NEW YORK, N. Y. 10003

TO THE

SUPERIOR

AND

THE OTHER SISTERS

OF

THE HOUSE OF MERCY AT
CLEWER,

WITH THANKFULNESS FOR THEIR PAST,
AND PRAYERS FOR THEIR FUTURE,
SUCCESS,

THESE HYMNS

ARE DEDICATED.

Sion's lyre, thou best content
That e'er Heav'n to mortals lent,
Though they as a trifle leave thee,
Whose dull thoughts cannot conceive thee,
Though to them thou be a scorn
Who to nought but earth are born,
May my life no longer be
Than I am in love with thee!

WITHER.

CONTENTS.

PREFACE.

THE following Translations have occupied
a portion of my leisure time for the last
twelve years : and some of them have
already appeared in more than one ecclesiastical periodical. So has also great part
of the Introduction.

It is a most remarkable fact, and one
which shows how very little interest has been
hitherto felt in the Eastern Church, that
these are literally, I believe, the only English
versions of any part of the treasures of
Oriental Hymnology. There is scarcely a
first or second-rate hymn of the Roman
Breviary which has not been translated : of
many we have six or eight versions. The

A

eighteen quarto volumes of Greek Church-poetry can only at present be known to the English reader by my little book.

Yet surely, if in the future Hymnal of the English Church we are to build an eclectic superstructure on the foundation of the Sarum Book, the East ought to yield its full share of compositions. And hence, I cannot but marvel that the compilers of eclectic Hymnals, such as the (modern) Sarum, the *Hymns, Ancient and Modern,* and others, have never turned to this source. Here was a noble field open to them; and to me it is incomprehensible that they should have so utterly neglected it.

There are difficulties in the task to which it is as well to advert. Though the superior terseness and brevity of the Latin Hymns renders a translation which shall represent those qualities a work of great labour, yet still the versifier has the help of the same metre; his version may be line for line; and there is a great analogy between the

Collects and the Hymns, most helpful to
the translator. Above all, we have examples enough of former translation by which
we may take pattern.

But in attempting a Greek Canon, from
the fact of its being in prose,—(metrical
Hymns, as the reader will learn, are unknown,)—one is all at sea. What measure
shall we employ? why this more than that?
Might we attempt the rhythmical prose of
the original, and design it to be chanted ?
Again, the great length of the Canons renders
them unsuitable for our churches, as *wholes*.
Is it better simply to form centos of the
more beautiful passages ? or can separate
Odes, each necessarily imperfect, be employed as separate Hymns ? And above all,
we have no pattern or example of any kind
to direct our labour.

These questions, and many others, have
as yet received no reply ; but will in time,
no doubt, work out their answer. My own
belief is, that the best way to employ Greek

Hymnology for the uses of the English Church, would be by centos.

The reader will find, in the following pages, examples of different methods of treatment. The following are short *Idiomela*, &c. which might serve as separate Hymns :

5. *The day is past and over.* (Evening.)

20. *O the mystery, passing wonder.* (Maundy Thursday.)

28. *Christian ! dost thou see them.* (A Sunday in Lent.)

35. *By fruit the ancient Foe's device.* (Easter Tide.)

65. *Those eternal bowers.* (All Saints.)

84. *The choirs of ransomed Israel.* (Transfiguration.)

124. *Are thy toils and woes increasing.* (Passion or Holy Week.)

Centos might perhaps be made from

The Canon for Easter,	p. 42.
,, Low Sunday,	p. 53.
,, Christmas,	p. 69.
,, Lent,	p. 24.
,, ,,	p. 107.

It has been with great thankfulness that I have seen such copious use made of my Mediæval Hymns, and my Rhythm of S. Bernard, in so many modern Hymnals. Permission has usually been most courteously asked: though in some few cases, whole Hymns have been taken without the slightest request for leave, or subsequent acknowledgment. I would therefore request any compiler of a Hymnal who may wish to quote from the following pages, to be so kind as first to express that wish to the publisher, or to myself.

I trust the reader will not forget the immense difficulty of an attempt so perfectly new as the present, where I have had no predecessors, and therefore could have no master. If I have opened the way for others to do better what I have done imperfectly, I shall have every reason to be thankful. I have kept most of the translations by me for at least the nine years recommended by Horace; and now offer them as

a contribution to the hymnology of our own
Church.   And while fully sensible of their
imperfections, I may yet (by way of excuse
rather than of boast) say, almost in Bishop
Hall's words—

> " I first adventure : foll w me who list,
>   And be the second Eastern Melodist."

SACKVILLE COLLEGE,
Feast of the Epiphany, 1862

INTRODUCTION.

As a general rule, the first poetical attempts
of the Eastern, like those of the Western,
Church, were in classical measures. But as
classical Greek died out from being a spoken
language,—as new trains of thought were
familiarized,—as new words were coined—a
versification became valueless, which was
attached with no living bonds to the new
energy, to the onward movement. Dean
Trench has admirably expressed this truth
in the introduction to his "Sacred Latin
Poetry," and showed how the "new wine
must be put into new bottles." Ecclesiastical terms *must* be used, which rebel
against classical metre: in Greek, no less
than in Latin, five words in eight would be
shut out of the principal classical rhythms.
Now, the Gospel was preached to the poor.
Church hymns must be the life-expression
of all hearts. The Church was forced to

make a way for saying in poetry what her message bade her say.*

---

* As an illustration of this remark, it is worth while noticing how very few examples of Hexameters occur in the New Testament. I believe that the following are all that are *tolerable*; that is, that can so be scanned without one or two false quantities :—

S. Luke xxi. 18.   Θρὶξ ἐκ τῆς κεφαλῆς ὑμῶν
        οὐ μὴ ἀπόληται.

S. John xiii. 5.   βάλλει ὕδωρ εἰς τὸν
        νιπτῆρα, καὶ ἤρξατο νίπτειν.

S. John xiii. 16.   οὐκ ἔστι[ν] δοῦλος μείζων
        τοῦ κυρίου αὐτοῦ.

S. John xvii. 20.   καὶ περὶ τῶν πιστευσόντων
        διὰ τοῦ λόγου αὐτῶν.

Titus iii. 2.   μηδένα βλασφημεῖν, ἀμάχους
        εἶναι, ἐπιεικεῖς.

Heb. xii. 13.   καὶ τροχιὰς ὀρθὰς ποιήσατε
        τοῖς ποσὶν ὑμῶν.

There are some which are very near a hexameter : as S. Matt xxiii. 6—
καὶ τὰς πρωτοκαθεδρίας ἐν ταῖς συναγωγαῖς.

A tolerable pentameter occurs in Rom. vi. 13—
    καὶ τὰ μέλη ὑμῶν ὅπλα δικαιοσύνης.

and a remarkable iambic in the LORD's Prayer—
    τὸν ἄρτον ἡμῶν τὸν ἐπιούσιον δίδου.

S. Gregory Nazianzen, the first Greek
Church poet, used only the ordinary classical measures. S. Sophronius of Jerusalem
employed (and in their way not unhappily,)
Anacreontics : and his hymns on various
festivals have some elegance. But there is
a certain degree of dilettante-ism, rather
than of earnestness, in these compositions ;
and the most airy, tripping, frivolous measure that the Greek Muse possessed, never,
by any possibility, could form the ordinary
utterance of the Church. The Church compositions of S. Sophronius, though called
ποιήματα, are in fact mere prose : as those
grand prayers on the Epiphany.

How then was the problem to be solved
as to the composition of Eastern Church
Song? In Latin, somewhat before the time
of S. Sophronius, A.D. 630, it was answered
by that glorious introduction of rhyme.
Why not in Greek also?

Now it is no less true in Greek, than in
Latin, that there was a tendency to rhyme

from the very beginning. Open Homer :
look for *caudate* rhymes :—

Νημερτής τε καὶ Ἀψευδὴς καὶ Καλλιάνασσα·
Ἔνθαδ' ἔην Κλυμένη, Ἰάνειρα καὶ
    Ἰφιάνασσα.   Il. xviii. 46.

Ἄστεος αἰθομένοιο· θεῶν δέ Ϝε μῆνις ἀνῆκεν·
Πᾶσι δὲ θῆκε πόνον· πολλοῖσι δὲ κήδε'
    ἐφῆκεν·
Ὡς Ἀχιλεὺς Τρώεσσι πόνον καὶ κήδεα θῆκεν.
                Il. xxi. 523.

Οὐ μὲν γὰρ μεῖζον κλέος ἀνέρος, ὄφρα κεν
    ἦσιν
Ἢ ὅ τι ποσσίν τε ῥέξει καὶ χερσὶ Ϝεῆσιν.
              Odyss. viii· 147.

Leonines are still more common. The
reader's attention is particularly requested
to those that follow :—

Il. ii. 220. Ἔχθιστος δ' Ἀχιλῆϊ μάλιστ'
        ἦν, ἠδ' Ὀδυσῆϊ.
    484. Ἔσπετε νῦν μοι, Μοῦσαι,
        Ὀλύμπια δώματ' ἔχουσαι.
    475. Ῥεῖα διακρίνωσιν, ἐπεί κε νομῷ
        μίγέωσιν.
  iii. 84. Ὡς ἔφαθ'· οἱ δ' ἔσχοντο μάχης,
        ἄνεῳ τ' ἐγένοντο.

v. 529. Ὦ φίλοι, ἀνέρες ἔστε, καὶ
ἄλκιμον ἦτορ ἔλεσθε.

vi. 242. Τὸν δ' Ἑλένη μύθοισι προσηύδα
μειλιχίοισι.

Od. i. 40. Ἐκ γὰρ Ὀρέσταο τίσις ἔσσεται
ἈτρεϜίδαο.

397. Αὐτὰρ ἐγὼ Ϝοίκοιο Ϝάναξ ἔσομ
ἡμετέροιο.

iv. 121. Ἐκ δ' Ἑλένη θαλάμοιο θυώδεος
ὑψορόφοιο.

xiv. 371. Ἀσπίδας, ὅσσαι ἄρισται ἐνὶ
στρατῷ ἠδὲ μέγισται.

And I might mark multitudes more : but
these are enough by way of example.   The
question then occurs at once, Why did not
the new life, instilled into the Greek as well
as into the Latin language by Christianity,
seize the grand capability of RHYME in the
one case as well as in the other?   How
stately it would have been in anapæstics!
how sweet in trochaics!   Why was it
neglected?

For this reason : the reader must remember that NONE OF THE RHYMES I HAVE

BEEN POINTING OUT IN HOMER WOULD
BE RHYMES TO A GREEK EAR. Read
them accentually, and you find ἄρισται and
μέγισται are no more double rhymes to a
Greek than *gloriously* and *ferociously* are
to us : μοῦσαι and ἔχουσαι, no more than
glory and *victory*. Accent, in the decline
of the language, was trampling down quantity. Now accent is not favourable to such
rhymes, though many poems have been
thus composed in the newer Greek :—

εὖρον φίλον κοματάκη
καθ᾽ ὅπερ τετραγωνάκη.

But it was not sufficiently removed from
every-day life,—too familiar,—had too little
dignity. There was an innate vulgarity
about it which rendered it impossible to the
Church.

Now, let it be observed, accentuation even
in Latin was not without its difficulty. In
the new style, dissyllables, whatever their
real quantity, were always read—and so we

read them now—as trochees. Férox, vélox, scéptrum. Hence a verse in the early metrical hymns, such as—

> " Castos fides somnos juvat,"

a dimeter iambic, would have been read in mediæval times, Cástos fídes sómnos júvat, and so have virtually become a dimeter trochaic.

Popular poetry soon devised its own metre, *political verse,* as it was called, because used for every-day domestic matters. This was none other than a favourite metre of Aristophanes, *iambic tetrameter catalectic,* —our own ballad rhythm :—

> " A Captain bold of Halifax, who lived in country quarters."

And this, sometimes with rhyme, sometimes without, is the favourite Romaic metre to the present day. For example :—

μὴ διὰ θύρας βαίνειν δὲ λέγω τοὺς κλεπταββάδας
χωστοὺς, ἐγκλείστους, ἔλκοντας θήρια, στελοβάτας,

πάντας ὅσοι παρὰ τὰ νόμιμα δρῶσι τὸν βίον,
και τῶν μονοτροπούντων δὲ, πλὴν ἐν ἐρήμου
τρόποις.

The Church never attempted this sing-
song stanza, and preferred falling back on
an older form.

From the brief allusions we find to the
subject in the New Testament, we should
gather that " the hymns and spiritual songs"
of the Apostles were written in metrical
prose. Accustomed as many of the early
Christians were to the Hebrew Scriptures,
this is not unlikely ; and proof seems strong
that it was so. Compare these passages :—

Eph. v. 14. Wherefore *he saith :* ἔγειρε ὁ
καθεύδων,
καὶ ἀνάστα ἐκ τῶν νεκρῶν·
ἐπιφαύσει σοι ὁ Χριστός.

Undoubtedly the fragment of a hymn.
Again :—

Apoc. iv. 8. μεγάλα καὶ θαυμαστὰ τὰ ἔργα
σου,
Κύριε ὁ Θεὸς, ὁ παντοκράτωρ·
δίκαιαι καὶ ἀληθιναὶ αἱ ὁδοί σου,
ὁ βασιλεὺς τῶν ἐθνῶν.

And nearly coeval with these we have the
Gloria in Excelsis, the *Ter Sanctus*, and
the *Joyful Light*.   Also the Eastern phase,
so to speak, of the *Te Deum*; the καθ'
ἑκάστην ἡμέραν.   And to this rhythmical
prose the Church now turned.

Then, not to pursue the subject with a
detail of which this Introduction will not
admit, we find that by the beginning of the
eighth century, verse, properly speaking
(and that with scarcely an exception), had
been discarded for ever from the hymns of
the Eastern Church; those hymns, occupy-
ing a space beyond all comparison greater
than they do in the Latin, being written in
measured prose.   And now to explain the
system.

The stanza which is to form the model of
the succeeding stanzas,—the strophe, in
fact,—is called the *Hirmos*, from its draw-
ing others after it.   The stanzas which are
to follow it are called *troparia*, from their
turning to it.

Let Ps. cxix. 13, be the Hirmos :—

> " I will talk of Thy commandments :
> and have respect unto Thy ways."

Then verse 15 would be a troparion to it :—

> " With my lips have I been telling :
> of all the judgments of Thy mouth."

So would 17 :—

> " O do well unto Thy servant :
> that I may live, and keep Thy word."

and Ps. cii. 16 :—

> " When the LORD shall build up Sion :
> and when His glory shall appear."

Let verse 44 be a Hirmos :

> " So shall I alway keep Thy law :
> yea, for ever and ever."

and 45 will be a troparion to it :—

> " And I will walk at liberty :
> for I seek Thy commandments."

These troparia are always divided for chanting by commas,—utterly irrespective of the sense. This separation into *commatisms* renders it very difficult to read them without practice. Take an example, with the corresponding effect in English :—

'Ωιδὴ ά. ἦχος δ'. ὁ εἱρμος.

Θαλάσσης τὸ ἐρυθραῖον πέλαγος, ἀβρόχοις ἴχνεσιν, ὁ παλαιὸς πεζεύσας Ἰσραὴλ, σταυροτύποις Μωσέως χερσὶ, τοῦ Ἀμαλὴκ τὴν δύναμιν, ἐν τῇ ἐρήμῳ ἐτροπώσατο.

"Israel in ancient times passing on foot with, unbedewed steps the Red Gulf, of the sea, turned to flight by, the cross-typifying arms, of Moses the might of Amalek, in the wilderness."

The perfection of troparia is in a Canon, of which I shall say more presently. I need not trouble the reader with the minute distinctions between *troparia* and *stichera;* as a *troparion* follows a *Hirmos,* so a *sticheron* follows an *homoion,* and then becomes a *prosomoion.* There are also *idiomela,*— that is, stanzas which are their own models, —and an infinite variety of names expressive of the different kind of troparia.

A A

A collection of any number of troparia, preceded by their Hirmos, sometimes merely quoted by its initial words, sometimes given at length, and with inverted commas, is an *Ode.*

Let the Hirmos be as before—

"With my lips have I," &c.

and the Ode might follow thus :—

Hirmos.

" With my lips have I been telling: of all the judgments of thy mouth.

" Let us break their bonds asunder: and cast away their cords from us.

" I am weary of my groaning and every night I wash my bed.

" For he lieth waiting secretly : as a lion in his den.

" I am poured out like water: and all my bones are out of joint."

Glory.

" I will talk of thy commandments: and have respect unto thy ways."

Both now.

And let this be most carefully observed :

an Ode is simply a *Sequence* under somewhat different laws. Just when the system of Greek ecclesiastical poetry was fully developed, S. Notker and the Monks of S. Gall hit out a similar one for the Latin Church: the Sequence or the Prose. It was not copied from the East, for we have S. Notker's own account of the way in which he invented it. It prospered to a certain extent; that is, it became one, though the least important, branch of Ecclesiastical verses.

Now the perfection of Greek poetry is attained by the Canons at Lauds, of which I proceed to speak.

A Canon consists of Nine Odes,—each Ode containing any number of troparia from three to beyond twenty. The reason for the number nine is this: that there are nine Scriptural canticles, employed at Lauds, (εἰς τὸν ῎Ορθρον), on the model of which those in every Canon are formed. The first: that of Moses after the passage of the Red

A A 2

Sea—the second, that of Moses in Deuteronomy (chap. xxxiii.)—the third, that of Hannah—the fourth, that of Habakkuk—the fifth, that of Isaiah (xxvi. 9—20)—the sixth, that of Jonah—the seventh, that of the Three Children, (verses 3—34, of our "Song" in the Bible Version)—the eighth, *Benedicite*—the ninth, *Magnificat* and *Benedictus*.

From this arrangement two consequences follow. The first, that, as the Second Canticle is never recited except in Lent, the Canons never have any second Ode. The second, that there is generally some reference, either direct or indirect, in each Ode, to the Canticle of the same number: in the first Ode, *e.g.*, to the Song of Moses at the Red Sea: in the third to that of Hannah. This gives rise, on the one hand, to a marvellous amount of ingenuity, in tracing the most far-fetched connexions—in discovering the most remote types;—it brings out into the clearest light the wonderful analogies which underlie the surface of Scripture narration; and so far imbues each Ode with a depth of Scriptural meaning which it could scarcely otherwise reach. On the other, it has a stiffening and cramping effect; and sometimes, especially to the uninitiated, has somewhat of a ludicrous tendency. It would be curious to sum up the variety of objects of which, in a thousand *Sixth Odes*, we find Jonah's Whale a type. On the whole, this custom has about the same disadvantages and advantages which Warton points out as resulting from the four rhymes of a Spenserian stanza ;—the advantages, — picturesqueness, ingenuity, discovery of new beauties: the disadvantages,—art not concealed by art, tautology, imparity of similitudes, a caricature of typology, painful and affected elaboration.

The Hirmos, on which each Ode is based, is sometimes quoted at length at the commencement, in which case it is always distinguished by inverted commas; or the first few words are merely cited as a note to the singer, for whose benefit the Tone is also given.

The next noticeable matter is that these Odes are usually arranged after an acrostich, itself commonly in verse : sometimes alphabetical. The latter device was probably borrowed from the Psalms; as for example, the 25, 112, 119.

The arrangement is not to be considered as an useless formality or *pretty-ism* : it was of the greatest importance, when so many Canons had to be remembered by heart. We know to what curious devices the Western Church, in matters connected with the Calendar, had recourse as a *Memoria Technica* ; and not a few of her short hymns were alphabetical, either by verses or by lines : I know no instance of any other kind of acrostich. Besides the line which forms the initials of Greek Canons, the name of the composer likewise finds a frequent place. And it is worth noticing that, whereas the authors of the world-famous hymns of the West, with a few exceptions (such as the *Vexilla Regis*, the *Dies Iræ*, the *Veni Sancte Spiritus*), are unknown, the case in the East is reversed. The acrostich may, or may not, run through the ⸸Theotokia, of which I now proceed to speak.

Each Ode is ended by a troparion, dedicated to the celebration of S. Mary, and thence named *Theotokion*. Sometimes there is another, which commemorates her at the Cross; and then it is a *Stauro-theotokion*. In long Canons, a stanza, sometimes intercalated at the end of the third or sixth Odes, is called a *Cathisma*, because the congregation are then allowed to sit. There is also the *Oicos*, literally the *House*,—which is the exact Italian *Stanza*,—about the length of three ordinary troparia. The *Catavasia* is a troparion in which both choirs come down together, and stand in the middle of the Church, singing it in common.

The acrostichs are usually in iambics,—
sometimes none of the best : *e.g.*—

ἐκπλήττομαί σου τοὺς λόγους, Ζαχαρία,

on the feast of S. Zacharias the Prophet :—
and generally bringing in some paronomasia
on the Saint's name ; as—

φερώνυμόν σε τοῦ Θεοῦ δῶρον σέβω, on

that of S. Dorotheus.

Or again :—

τρυφῆς μεθέξειν ἀξίωσόν με, Τρύφων·

and of S. Clement :—

μέλπω σε, κλῆμα τῆς νοητῆς ἀμπέλου.

But there are examples of acrostichs which
take the form of an hexameter, as—

εἰκάδι οὐρανοῦ εἰς ξενίην Ξένη ἦλθε
τετάρτῃ.

τὸν πανάριστον ἐν ᾿ασκηταῖς Μακάριον
κυδάινω·

and

Τιμόθεον τὸν Ἀπόστολον ᾀσμασι τοῖσδε γεραίρω·

and

τὸν θεορήμονα Γρηγόριον τὸν ἀοίδιμον ᾄδω.

I shall more than once have occasion to observe that, while the earlier Odes, which treat of such subjects as the Resurrection, Ascension, Nativity, are magnificent specimens of religious poetry, the later ones, composed in commemoration of martyrs, of whom nothing but the fact of their martyrdom is known, are often grievously dull and heavy. Herein the Eastern Church would have done well; to have had, for such as these, a Canon of the Common of Martyrs, instead of celebrating each differently;—if the tautology which composes such Odes can indeed be called *different*.

I said, some short time since, that the Greek Ode and the Latin Notkerian Sequence were essentially the same. This being so, it is to introduce confusion into the very axioms of hymnology to call that kind of

Sequence, as Mone does, Troparia. The Troparion does not answer to the Sequence, but to each stanza of the Sequence. The differences between Odes and Sequences may briefly be summed up as follows:—

1. The *Hirmos* in the former has a number of Troparia following it and based on it, whereas in the latter the *Troparia* run in couples; that is, one *Hirmos* has one follower, or *troparion*, and there an end; then another follows another, and so on. There are sometimes triplets, but these are not common.

2. The *Hirmos* in Greek Odes is always an already existing Troparion; whereas, in Latin, the writer generally composed that as much as any other part of the Sequence. But in certain Sequences this was not always the case. Godeschalkus sometimes took a verse from the Psalms.

3. Sometimes, indeed, a whole Sequence was made *super* some other Sequence, and then it became a vast Troparion, the different

verses taking the place of the *commatisms* in Greek Odes.   In the February number of *The Ecclesiologist* for 1859, is given a list of Hirmos-Sequences, from the Brander MS. of S. Gall.   But even in these cases, it is better not to call them Troparia, as they have so little real resemblance to Greek stanzas of that kind: I had rather see them called Homoia.

4. The rhythm in the Greek is far more exact.   Not only the syllabic arrangement, but the accentuation is the same; whereas in Latin, the accentuation is often *counter ;* that is, an iambic dimeter in the Hirmos is answered by a trochaic dimeter in the Troparion.   For example, if the Hirmos were,—

> " The LORD is great in Sion :
> and high above all people,"

the requirements of a Sequence would be satisfied with the Troparion,

> " Look upon my misery :
> and forgive me all my sins."

Such a licence would not for one moment be allowed in the Greek.

I next have to speak of the books in which Greek Hymnology is to be found. They consist principally of sixteen volumes.

a. Twelve of the *Menœa :*—which would answer, in Western Ritual, to the Breviary, minus the ferial offices. But, whereas in the West, the only human compositions of the Breviary are the lections from the sermons of the Fathers, the hymns, and a few responses—the body of the Eastern Breviary is ecclesiastical poetry : poetry, not strictly speaking written in verse, but in measured prose. This is the staple of those three thousand pages—under whatever name the stanzas may be presented—forming Canons and Odes ; as Troparia, Idiomela, Stichera, Stichoi, Contakia, Cathismata, Theotokia, Triodia, Staurotheotokia, Catavasiai,—or whatever else. Nine-tenths of the Eastern Service-book is poetry.

β The *Paracletice,* or *Great Octoechus :* in eight parts.

This contains the Ferial Office for eight weeks.   Each week has on Sunday—

A Canon of the Trinity.

——— Resurrection.

——— Cross and Resurrection.

——— Mother of GOD (one or more.)

On Monday :

——— of Penitence.

——— of the Angels.

On Tuesday :

——— of Penitence.

——— of the Forerunner.

On Wednesday :

——— of the Cross.

——— of the Mother of GOD.

On Thursday :

——— of the Apostles.

——— of S. Nicolas.

On Friday :

——— of the Passion.

——— of the Mother of GOD, (two.)

On Saturday :

——— of Prophets & Martyrs.

——— of the Dead.

In the first week, the whole of the Canons are sung to the first Tone: in the second, to the second, and so on. The Greek Tones answer to our Gregorian, thus :—

Latin.	Greek.	
Tone I.	I.	The *Paracletice* forms
II.	I. Plagal.	a quarto volume
III.	II.	(double columns)
IV.	II. Plagal.	of 350 pages : at
V.	III.	least half is the
VI.	Varys (heavy.)	work of Joseph of
VII.	IV.	the Studium. The
VIII.	IV. Plagal.	*Octoechus*, some-
		times called the

Little Octoechus, are the Sunday services from the Paracletice: they are often printed separately.

γ. The *Triodion*: the Lent volume, which commences on the Sunday of the Pharisee and Publican (that before Septuagesima) and goes down to Easter. It is so called, because the leading Canons have, during that period, only three Odes.

δ. The *Pentecostarion*,—more properly the *Pentecostarion Charmosynon*,—the Office for Easter-tide. On a moderate compution, these volumes together comprise 5,000 closely printed quarto pages, in double columns, of which at least 4,000 are poetry.

The thought that, in conclusion, strikes one is this : the marvellous ignorance in which English ecclesiastical scholars are content to remain of this huge treasure of divinity— the gradual completion of nine centuries at least. I may safely calculate that not one out of twenty who peruse these pages will ever have read a Greek '*Canon*' through ; yet what a glorious mass of theology do these offices present ! If the following pages tend in any degree to induce the reader to study these books for himself, my labour could hardly have been spent to a better result.

EPOCHS OF
GREEK ECCLESIASTICAL POETRY.

LIKE that of the Latin, the Poetry of the Greek Church may be divided into three epochs:—

I. That of *formation*, while it was gradually throwing off the bondage of classical metres, and inventing and perfecting its various styles; and this ends about A.D. 726.

II. That of *perfection* : which, as we shall see, nearly coincides with the period of the Iconoclastic Controversy, A.D. 726-820.

III. That of *decadence* : when the effeteness of an effeminate Court, and the dissolution of a decaying Empire, reduced ecclesiastical poetry, by slow degrees, to a stilted bombast, giving great words to little meaning, heaping up epithet on epithet, tricking out commonplaces in diction more and more gorgeous, till sense and simplicity are alike sought in vain. A.D. 820-1400.

FIRST EPOCH.
A.D. 360....A.D. 726.

It is not my intention to dwell on the hymn writers of this period, as S. Gregory Nazianzen and S. Sophronius, because their works have not been employed in the Divine office, are merely an imitation of classical writers, and, however occasionally pretty, are not the stuff out of which Church song is made. There is but one writer in this epoch who gives spring-promise of the approaching summer, and that is S. Anatolius.

S. Anatolius.

d. 458.

The first poet who emancipated himself from the tyranny of old laws—hence to be compared to Venantius Fortunatus in the West—and who boldly struck out the new path of harmonious prose, was S. Anatolius of Constantinople. His commencements were not promising. He had been *apocrisiarius*, or legate, from the arch-heretic Dioscorus, to the Emperor's Court: and at the death of S. Flavian, in consequence of the violence received in the *"Robbers' Meeting"* at Ephesus, A.D. 449, he was, by the influence of his Pontiff, raised to the vacant throne of Constantinople. He soon, however, vindicated his orthodoxy: and, in the Council of Chalcedon, he procured the enactment of the famous 28th Canon, by which, (in spite of all the efforts of Rome,) Constantinople was raised to the second place among Patriarchal Sees. Having governed his Church eight years in peace, he departed to his rest in A.D. 458. His compositions are not numerous, and are almost all short, but they are usually very spirited.

STICHERA FOR A SUNDAY OF THE FIRST TONE.

ζοφερᾶς τρικυμίας.

Fierce was the wild billow;
　Dark was the night;
Oars labour'd heavily;
　Foam glimmer'd white;
Mariners trembled;
　Peril was nigh;
Then said the GOD of GOD,
　—"Peace! It is I!"

Ridge of the mountain-wave,
　Lower thy crest!
Wail of Euroclydon,
　Be thou at rest!
Peril can none be,—
　Sorrow must fly,—
Where saith the Light of Light,
　—"Peace! It is I!"

JESU, Deliverer!
　Come Thou to me:
Soothe Thou my voyaging
　Over Life's sea!
Thou, when the storm of Death
　Roars, sweeping by,
Whisper, O Truth of Truth!
　—"Peace! It is I!"

EVENING HYMN.

τὴν ἡμέραν διελθών.

This little hymn, which, I believe, is not used in the public service of the Church, is a great favourite in the Greek Isles. It is attributed to *an* Anatolius; and its evident antiquity may well lead to the belief that it is the work of our present author. It is to the scattered hamlets of Chios and Mitylene, what Bishop Ken's Evening Hymn is to the villages of our own land; and its melody is singularly plaintive and soothing.

The day is past and over :
　All thanks, O LORD, to Thee !
I pray Thee now, that sinless
　The hours of dark may be.
O JESU ! keep me in Thy sight,
And save me through the coming night !

The joys of day are over :
   I lift my heart to Thee ;
And ask Thee, that offenceless
   The hours of dark may be.
O JESU! make their darkness light,
And save me through the coming night !

The toils of day are over :
   I raise the hymn to Thee;
And ask that free from peril
   The hours of dark may be.
O JESU ! keep me in Thy sight,
And guard me through the coming night !

Lighten mine eyes, O SAVIOUR,
   Or sleep in death shall I ;
And he, my wakeful tempter,
   Triumphantly shall cry :
" He could not make their darkness light,
Nor guard them through the hours of
    night !"

Be Thou my soul's preserver,
   O GOD ! for Thou dost know
How many are the perils
   Through which I have to go :
Lover of men ! O hear my call,
And guard and save me from them all !

S. STEPHEN'S DAY.

—

STICHERA AT VESPERS.

—

Τῷ Βασιλεῖ καὶ Δεσπότῃ.

The LORD and King of all things
   But yesterday was born :
And Stephen's glorious off'ring
   His birthtide shall adorn.
No pearls of orient splendour,
   No jewels can he show ;
But with his own true heart's blood
   His shining vestments glow.

Come, ye that love the Martyrs,
   And pluck the flow'rs of song,
And weave them in a garland
   For this our suppliant throng :
And cry,—O Thou that shinest
   In grace's brightest ray,
CHRIST's valiant Protomartyr,
   For peace and favour pray !

Thou first of all Confessors,
    Of all the Deacons crown,
Of every following athlete
    The glory and renown :
Make supplication, standing
    Before CHRIST'S Royal Throne,
That He would give the Kingdom,
    And for our sins atone !

[In contrast with the above Stanzas, the reader may not be displeased to compare the celebrated sequence of Adam of S. Victor, *Heri mundus exultavit ;* which has never yet, I believe, appeared in English.]

HERI MUNDUS EXULTAVIT.

Yesterday, with exultation
Join'd the world in celebration
    Of her promis'd Saviour's birth :
Yesterday the Angel nation
Pour'd the strains of jubilation
    O'er the Monarch born on earth.

But to-day, o'er death victorious,
By his faith and actions glorious,
  By his miracles renown'd,
Dared the Deacon Protomartyr
Earthly life for Heav'n to barter,
  Faithful midst the faithless found.

Forward, champion, in thy quarrel !
Certain of a certain laurel,
  Holy Stephen, persevere !
Perjur'd witnesses confounding,
Satan's Synagogue astounding
  By thy doctrine true and clear.

Lo ! in Heav'n thy Witness liveth ;
Bright and faithful proof He giveth
  Of His Martyr's full success :
Thou by name *a Crown* impliest ;
Meetly then in pangs thou diest
  For the Crown of Righteousness !

For a crown that fadeth never,
Bear the torturer's brief endeavour,
  Victory waits to end the strife.

Death shall be thy birth's beginning,
And life's losing be the winning
   Of a true and better life.

Whom the HOLY GHOST endueth,
Whom celestial sight imbueth,
   Stephen penetrates the skies :
There GOD's fullest glory viewing,
There his victor strength renewing,
   For his near reward he sighs.

See, as Jewish foes invade thee,
See, how JESUS *stands* to aid thee :
   Stands, to guard His champion's death !
Cry that opened Heav'n is shown thee :
Cry that JESUS waits to own thee :
   Cry it with thy latest breath !

As the dying Martyr kneeleth,
For his murderers he appealeth,
And his prayer their pardon sealeth,
   For their madness grieving sore ;
Then in CHRIST he sleepeth sweetly,
Who His pattern kept completely,
And with CHRIST he reigneth meetly,
   Martyr first-fruits, evermore !

STICHERA FOR CHRISTMAS-TIDE.

μέγα καὶ παράδοξον θαῦμα.

A great and mighty wonder,
  The festal makes secure :
The Virgin bears the Infant
  With Virgin-honour pure.

The Word is made Incarnate,
  And yet remains on high :
And Cherubim sing anthems
  To shepherds from the sky.

And we with them triumphant
  Repeat the hymn again :
" To GOD on high be glory,
  And peace on earth to men ! "

While thus they sing your Monarch,
  Those bright angelic bands;
Rejoice, ye vales and mountains !
  Ye oceans, clap your hands !

Since all He comes to ransom,
    By all be He adored,
The Infant born in Bethlehem,
    The Saviour and the LORD !

And idol forms shall perish,
    And error shall decay,
And CHRIST shall wield His sceptre,
    Our LORD and GOD for aye.

IDIOMELON FOR CHRISTMAS.

ἐν Βηθλεέμ.

In Bethlehem is He born,
Maker of all things, everlasting GOD!
He opens Eden's gate,
Monarch of Ages!   Thence the fiery sword
Gives glorious passage ; thence
That severing mid-wall overthrown, the
Powers
Of earth and Heav'n are one :
Angels and men renew their ancient league,
The pure rejoin the pure
In happy union!   Now the Virgin-womb,
Like some Cherubic throne,
Containeth Him, the Uncontainable :
Bears Him, Whom while *they* bear
The Seraphs tremble: bears Him, as He
comes
To shower upon the world
The fulness of His everlasting love.

SECOND EPOCH.

A.D. 726.... A.D. 820.

———

The second period of Greek Hymnology is very nearly, as I said, coincident with the Iconoclastic controversy. Its first writer, indeed, died shortly after the commencement of that stormy age, and took no share in its Councils nor sufferings; while the last hymnographer who bore a part in its proceedings, S. Joseph of the Studium, belongs to the decline of his art. With these two exceptions, the ecclesiastical poets of this period were not only thrown into the midst of that great struggle, but, with scarcely one exception, took an active share in it.

A few words on that conflict of one hundred and sixteen years are absolutely necessary, if we would understand the progress

and full development of Greek Hymno-
graphy. No controversy has been more
grossly misapprehended ; none, without the
key of subsequent events, could have been
so difficult to appreciate. Till Calvinism,
and its daughter Rationalism, showed the
ultimate development of Iconoclast prin-
ciples, it must have been well-nigh impossible to realize the depth of feeling on
the side of the Church, or the greatness of
the interests attacked by her opponents.
We may perhaps doubt whether even the
Saints of that day fully understood the
character of the battle ; whether they did
not give up ease, honour, possessions, life
itself, rather from an intuitive perception
that their cause was the cause of the Cátholic
faith, than from a logical induction of the
results to which the Image-destroyers were
tending. Just so, in the early part of the
Nestorian controversy, many and many a
simple soul felt intuitively that the title of
the *Theotocos* was to be defended, without
seeing the full consequences to which its

denial would subsequently lead. The supporters of Icons, by universal consent, numbered amongst their ranks all that was pious and venerable in the Eastern Church. The Iconoclasts seem to have been the legitimate development of that secret creeping Manichæism, which, under the various names of Turlupins, Bogomili, or Goodmen, so long devasted CHRIST's fold.

We must keep the landmarks of the controversy in sight. Commenced by Leo the Isaurian, in A.D. 726, the persecution was carried on by his despicable son, Constantine Copronymus, who also endeavoured to destroy monasticism. The great Council of Constantinople, attended by 338 prelates, in 752, which rejected the use of images, was the culminating success of the Iconoclasts. Lulling at the death of Constantine, the persecution again broke out in the latter years of his successor Leo, and was only terminated by the death of that prince, and the succession of Constantine and Irene. The Second Council of Nicæa, seventh

Œcumenical (A.D. 787), attended by 377 Bishops, seemed to end the heresy; but it again broke out under the Iconoclast Emperor, Leo the Armenian (813), and after having been carried on under the usurper Michael, and his son Theophilus, ended with the death of the latter in 842. In the Hymnographers of this epoch, it may be noticed that the Second Council of Nicæa forms the culminating point of ecclesiastical poetry. Up to that date, there is a vigour and freshness which the twenty-eight years of peace succeeding the Council corrupted, and that rapidly, with the fashionable language of an effete court, and deluged with Byzantine bombast.

S. Andrew of Crete.

A.D. 660....A.D. 732.

———

Andrew was born at Damascus, about the year 660, and embraced the monastic life at Jerusalem, from which city he sometimes takes his name. Hence he was sent on ecclesiastical business to Constantinople, where he became a Deacon of the Great Church, and Warden of the Orphanage. His first entrance on public life does no credit to his sanctity. During the reign of Philippicus Bardanes, (711—714) he was raised by that usurper to the Archiepiscopate of Crete; and shortly afterwards was one of the Pseudo-Synod of Constantinople, held under the Emperor's auspices in A.D. 712, and which condemned the Sixth Œcumenical Council, and restored the Monothelite heresy.

At a late period, however, he returned to the faith of the Church, and refuted the error into which he had fallen. Seventeen of his Homilies, rather laboured than eloquent, remain to us: that in which he rises highest is, not unnaturally, his sermon on S. Titus, Apostle of Crete. He died in the island of Hierissus, near Mitylene, about the year 732.

As a poet, his most ambitious composition is the Great Canon; which, partially used during other days of Lent, is sung right through on the Thursday of Mid-Lent week, called, indeed, from that hymn. His Triodia in Holy Week, and Canons on Mid-Pentecost are fine; and he has a great variety of spirited Idiomela scattered through the *Triodion* and *Pentecostarion.*

STICHERA FOR GREAT THURSDAY.

τὸ μέγα μυστήριον.

O the mystery, passing wonder,
   When, reclining at the board,
" Eat," Thou saidst to Thy Disciples,
   "That True Bread with quickening stored:
" Drink in faith the healing chalice
   "From a dying GOD outpoured."

Then the glorious upper chamber
   A celestial tent was made,
When the bloodless rite was offered,
   And the soul's true service paid,
And the table of the feasters
   As an altar stood displayed.

CHRIST is now our mighty Pascha,
   Eaten for our mystic bread :
As a lamb led out to slaughter,
   And for this world offered :
Take we of His broken body,
   Drink we of the Blood He shed.

To the Twelve spake Truth eternal,
　To the Branches spake the Vine :
Never more from this day forward
　Shall I taste again this wine,
Till I drink it in the kingdom
　Of my FATHER, and with Mine.

Thou hast stretched those hands for silver
　That had held the immortal food ;
With those lips that late had tasted
　Of the Body and the Blood,
Thou hast given the kiss, O Judas;
　Thou hast heard the woe bestowed.

CHRIST to all the world gives banquet
　On that most celestial meat :
Him, albeit with lips all earthly,
　Yet with holy hearts we greet :
Him, the sacrificial Pascha,
　Priest and Victim all complete.

TROPARIA FOR PALM SUNDAY.

The following Stanzas are from the Triodion sung
at Compline on Palm Sunday; which has the same
name among the Greeks as among ourselves.

Ἰησοῦς ὑπὲρ τοῦ κόσμου

JESUS, hastening for the world to suffer,
 Enters in, Jerusalem, to thee:
With His Twelve He goeth forth to offer
 That free Sacrifice He came to be.

They that follow Him with true affection
 Stand prepared to suffer for His Name:
Be we ready then for man's rejection,
 For the mockery, the reproach, the shame.

Now in sorrow, sorrow finds its healing:
 In the form wherein our father fell,
CHRIST appears, those quick'ning Wounds
  revealing,
 Which shall save from sin and death and
  hell.

Now, Judæa, call thy Priesthood nigh thee!
  Now for Deicide prepare thy hands!
Lo thy Monarch, meek and gentle, by thee!
  Lo! the Lamb and Shepherd in thee
    stands!

To thy monarch, Salem, give glad greeting!
  Willingly He hastens to be slain,
For the multitude His entrance meeting
  With their false Hosanna's ceaseless strain.
    Blest is He that comes, they cry,
    On the Cross for man to die!

THE GREAT CANON.

—

It would be unpardonable not to give a portion of that which the Greeks regard as the king of Canons—the Great Canon of the Mid-Lent week. It is a collection of Scriptural examples, turned to the purpose of penitential Confession. It is impossible to deny the beauty of many stanzas, and the ingenuity of some tropological applications. But the immense length of the Canon, for it exceeds three hundred stanzas, and its necessary tautology, must render it wearisome, unless devotionally used under the peculiar circumstances for which it is appointed. The following is a part of the earlier portion.

Πόθεν ἄρξομαι θρηνεῖν.

Whence shall my tears begin?
What first-fruits shall I bear
Of earnest sorrow for my sin?
Or how my woes declare?
Oh Thou! the Merciful and Gracious One!
Forgive the foul transgressions I have done.

With Adam I have vied,
   Yea, pass'd him, in my fall;
  And I am naked now, by pride
   And lust made bare of all;
Of Thee, O GOD, and that Celestial Band,
And all the glory of the Promised Land.

   No earthly Eve beguil'd
   My body into sin:
  A spiritual temptress smiled,
   Concupiscence within:
Unbridled passion grasp'd the unhallow'd
   sweet:
Most bitter—ever bitter—was the meat.

   If Adam's righteous doom,
   Because he dared transgress
  Thy one decree, lost Eden's bloom
   And Eden's loveliness:
What recompense, O LORD, must I expect,
Who all my life Thy quickening laws
   neglect?

By mine own act, like Cain,
    A murderer was I made :
By mine own act my soul was slain,
    When Thou wast disobeyed :
And lusts each day are quickened, warring
        still
Against the soul with many a deed of ill.

Thou formed'st me of clay,
    O Heav'nly Potter !   Thou
In fleshly vesture didst array,
    With life and breath endow.
Thou Who didst make, didst ransom, and
        dost know,
To Thy repentant creature pity show !

My guilt for vengeance cries ;
    But yet Thou pardonest all,
And whom Thou lov'st Thou dost chastise,
    And mourn'st for them that fall :
Thou, as a Father, mark'st our tears and
        pain,
And welcomest the prodigal again.

I lie before Thy door,
  O turn me not away !
Nor in mine old age give me o'er
  To Satan for a prey !
But ere the end of life and term of grace,
Thou Merciful ! my many sins efface !

  The Priest beheld, and pass'd
  The way he had to go :
A careless glance the Levite cast,
  And left me to my woe :
But Thou, O JESU, Mary's SON, console,
Draw nigh, and succour me, and make me
    whole !

  Thou Spotless Lamb divine,
  Who takest sin away,
Remove far off the load that mine
  Upon my conscience lay :
And, of Thy tender mercy, grant thou me
To find remission of iniquity !

STICHERA FOR THE SECOND WEEK
OF THE GREAT FAST.

———

οὐ γὰρ βλέπεις τοὺς ταράττοντας.

Christian ! dost thou *see* them
   On the holy ground,
How the troops of Midian
   Prowl and prowl around ?
Christian ! up and smite them,
   Counting gain but loss :
Smite them by the merit
   Of the Holy Cross !

Christian ! dost thou *feel* them,
   How they work within,
Striving, tempting, luring,
   Goading into sin ?
Christian ! never tremble !
   Never be down-cast !
Smite them by the virtue
   Of the Lenten Fast !

Christian ! dost thou *hear* them,
   How they speak thee fair ?
Always fast and vigil ?
   Always watch and prayer ?
Christian ! answer boldly :
   While I breathe I pray :
Peace shall follow battle,
   Night shall end in day.

" Well I know thy trouble,
   O My servant true ;
Thou art very weary,—
   I was weary too :
But that toil shall make thee
   Some day, all Mine own :
But the end of sorrow
   Shall be near My Throne."

MESO-PENTECOST.

———

The day which halves the distance between Easter and Pentecost, is a feast of no small dignity in the Oriental Church; and the Canon at lauds is the composition of our present poet. I will try a portion of it in rhymeless lyric metre, which, to my own mind, gives the truest representation of the original.

ODE I.

Thou turnedst the Sea.

Exult, ye Gentiles! mourn, ye Hebrews!
    CHRIST,
    Giver of Life, hath burst
    The fetters of the Tomb :
And rais'd the dead again, and heal'd the
    sick.
  This is our GOD, Who giveth health
To every soul believing on His Name.

Marvel of marvels !   Thou, O LORD, didst
     turn
    The water into wine,
    As once Thou spak'st the word
To Egypt's river, and forthwith 'twas blood.
    All praise to Thee, O LORD, Who now
By laying down Thy glory, man renew'st !

O overflowing stream of truest life,
     Our Resurrection, LORD !
    Thou for our sakes didst toil,
Thou for our sakes—so Nature will'd—didst
     thirst :
    And resting Thee by Sichar's well,
Of the Samaritan didst seek to drink.

Thou blessest bread, Thou multipliest fish,
     Incomprehensible !
    Thou freely feed'st the crowd,
And givest Wisdom's spring to thirsting
     men.
    Thou art our SAVIOUR, O our GOD !
Giver of Life to them that trust in Thee !

Glory.

Three co-eternal, co-enthroned, I laud :
    The Unbegotten SIRE,
    And Co-existent SON,
And SPIRIT, co-eternal with the Twain :
    Tri-hypostatic Essence !   One
In might and majesty and Godhead sole.

Both now.

Mother of GOD !   Thou only didst contain
    The Uncontainable ;
    And brought'st the Infant forth,
Ineffable in Thy Virginity.
    Hence without ceasing, O most pure,
Vouchsafe to call down blessing on Thy
    flock !

Catavasia.

Thou turn'd'st the sea to land, when Thou
    didst whelm
    Pharaoh and all his host,
    His chariot and his horse :
And ledd'st Thy people to the Holy Mount.
    Sing we, said they, to Thee our GOD,
Mighty in war, this Ode of Victory !

S. Germanus.

A.D. 634.......A.D. 734.

S. Germanus of Constantinople, was born
in that city about 634. His father, Justinian,
a patrician, had the ill-fortune to excite
the jealousy of the Emperor Constantine
Pogonatus, who put him to death, and
obliged Germanus to enrol himself among
the Clergy of the Great Church. Here he
became distinguished for piety and learning,
and in process of time was made Bishop of
Cyzicus. In this capacity he assisted, with
S. Andrew of Crete, in the Synod of Constantinople of which I have just spoken;
and no doubt, he might be the more favor-
ably disposed to Monotheletism, because he
had been so deeply injured by its great
opponent, Pogonatus. However, he also,
at a late period, expressly condemned that
heresy. Translated to the throne of Constantinople in 715, he governed his Patriar-

D

chate in tranquillity. On the attack of
Leo the Isaurian against Icons, his letters,
in opposition to the Imperial mandate, were
the first warnings of the impending storm
which the Church received. Refusing to
sign the decrees of the Synod which was
convoked by that Emperor in A.D. 730,
and stripping off his Patriarchal robes,
with the words—"It is impossible for me,
Sire, to innovate, without the sanction of
the Œcumenical Council," he was driven
from his See, not, it is said, without blows,
and returned to his own house at Platanias,
where he thenceforth led a quiet and private
life. He died shortly afterwards, aged about
one hundred years, and is regarded by the
Greeks as one of their most glorious Confessors.

The poetical compositions of S. Germanus
are few.

He has stanzas on S. Simon Stylites, on
the Prophet Elias, and on the Decollation
of S. John Baptist. His most poetical work
is perhaps his Canon on the Wonder-working

Image in Edessa. But probably the following simpler stanzas, for Sunday in the
Week of the First Tone, will better com-
mend themselves to the English reader.

By fruit, the ancient Foe's device
Drave Adam forth from Paradise:
CHRIST, by the Cross of shame and pain,
Brought back the dying Thief again:
" When in Thy kingdom, LORD," said he,
" Thou shalt return, remember me!"

Thy Holy Passion we adore
And Resurrection, evermore:
With heart and voice to Thee on high,
As Adam and the Thief, we cry:
" When in Thy kingdom Thou shalt be
" Victor o'er all things, think of me!"

Thou, after three appointed days,
Thy Body's Temple did'st upraise:
And Adam's children, one and all,
With Adam, to New Life didst call.
" When Thou," they cry, " shalt Victor be,
" In that Thy kingdom, think of me!"

Early, O CHRIST, to find Thy Tomb,
The weeping Ointment-bearers come:
The Angel, cloth'd in white, hath said,
" Why seek the LIVING with the dead?
"The LORD of Life hath burst death's chain,
" Whom here ye weep and seek in vain."

The Apostles, on Thy Vision bent,
To that appointed mountain went:
And there they worship when they see,
And there the Message comes from Thee,
That every race beneath the skies
They should disciple and baptise.

We praise the FATHER, GOD on High,
The Holy SON we magnify:
Nor less our praises shall adore
The HOLY GHOST for evermore;
This grace, Blest TRINITY, we crave;
Thy suppliant servants hear and save!

S. John Damascene.

Died circ. A.D. 780.

S. John Damascene has the double honor of being the last but one of the Fathers of the Eastern Church, and the greatest of her poets. It is surprising, however, how little is known of his life. That he was born of a good family at Damascus,—that he made great progress in philosophy,—that he administered some charge under the Caliph, that he retired to the monastery of S. Sabas, in Palestine,—that he was the most learned and eloquent with whom the Iconoclasts had to contend,—that at a comparatively late period of life he was ordained Priest of the Church of Jerusalem, and that he died after 754, and before 787, seems to comprise

all that has reached us of his biography
His enemies, from an unknown reason,
called him *Mansur;* whether he were the
same with John Arklas, also an ecclesiastical
poet, is not so certain.

As a poet, he had a principal share in the
Octoechus, of which I have already spoken.
His three Great Canons are those on Easter,
the Ascension, and S. Thomas's Sunday,
which I shall give either wholly or in part.
Probably, however, many of the Idiomela
and Stichera which are scattered about the
office-books under the title of *John,* and
John the Hermit, are his. His eloquent
defence of Icons, has deservedly procured
him the title of *The Doctor of Christian
Art.*

CANON FOR EASTER DAY,

CALLED

THE GOLDEN CANON,

OR,

THE QUEEN OF CANONS.

The circumstances under which the Canon is sung are thus eloquently described by a modern writer. The scene is at Athens.

"As midnight approached, the Archbishop, with his priests, accompanied by the King and Queen, left the Church, and stationed themselves on the platform, which was raised considerably from the ground, so that they were distinctly seen by the people. Everyone now remained in breathless expectation, holding their unlighted tapers in readiness when the glad moment should arrive, while the priests still continued murmuring their melancholy chant in a low half-whisper. Suddenly a single

report of a cannon announced that twelve
o'clock had struck, and that Easter day had
begun; then the old Archbishop elevating
the cross, exclaimed in a loud exulting tone,
'Christos anesti, CHRIST is risen!' and
instantly every single individual of all that
host took up the cry, and the vast multitude
broke through and dispelled for ever the
intense and mournful silence which they
had maintained so long, with one spontaneous shout of indescribable joy and
triumph, 'CHRIST is risen!' 'CHRIST is
risen!' At the same moment, the oppress-
ive darkness was succeeded by a blaze of
light from thousands of tapers, which com-
municating one from another, seemed to
send streams of fire in all directions, render-
ing the minutest objects distinctly visible,
and casting the most vivid glow on the
expressive faces, full of exultation, of the
rejoicing crowd; bands of music struck up
their gayest strains; the roll of the drum
through the town, and further on the peal-
ing of the cannon announced far and near

these 'glad tidings of great joy;' while from hill and plain, from the sea-shore and the far olive grove, rocket after rocket ascending to the clear sky, answered back with their mute eloquence, that CHRIST is risen indeed, and told of other tongues that were repeating those blessed words, and other hearts that leapt for joy; everywhere men clasped each other's hands, and congratulated one another, and embraced with countenances beaming with delight, as though to each one separately some wonderful happiness had been proclaimed;— and so in truth it was;—and all the while, rising above the mingling of many sounds, each one of which was a sound of gladness, the aged priests were distinctly heard chanting forth a glorious old hymn of victory in tones so loud and clear, that they seemed to have regained their youth and strength to tell the world how 'CHRIST is risen from the dead, having trampled death beneath His feet, and henceforth the entombed have everlasting life.'"

That which follows is the "Glorious old Hymn of Victory."

ODE I.

ἀναστάσεως ἡμέρα.

'Tis the Day of Resurrection :
    Earth ! tell it out abroad !
The Passover of Gladness !
    The Passover of GOD !
From Death to Life Eternal,—
    From earth unto the sky,
Our CHRIST hath brought us over,
    With hymns of victory.

Our hearts be pure from evil,
    That we may see aright
The LORD in rays eternal
    Of Resurrection-Light :
And, listening to His accents,
    May hear, so calm and plain,
His own—*All Hail !*—and hearing,
    May raise the victor strain !

Now let the Heav'ns be joyful !
  Let earth her song begin !
Let the round world keep triumph,
  And all that is therein :
Invisible and visible
  Their notes let all things blend,—
For CHRIST the LORD hath risen,—
  Our Joy That hath no end.

ODE III.

Δεῦτε πόμα πίωμεν.

Come and let us drink of that New River,
  Not from barren Rock divinely poured,
But the Fount of Life that is for ever
  From the Sepulchre of CHRIST the LORD.

All the world hath bright illumination,—
  Heav'n and Earth and things beneath the
    earth :
'Tis the Festival of all Creation :
  CHRIST hath ris'n, Who gave Creation
    birth.

Yesterday with Thee in burial lying,
  Now to-day with Thee aris'n I rise ;
Yesterday the partner of Thy dying,
  With Thyself upraise me to the skies.

ODE IV.

ἐπὶ τῆς θέιας φυλακῆς.

Stand on thy watch-tower, Habakkuk the
　　　　Seer,
And show the Angel, radiant in his light :
To-day, saith he, Salvation shall appear,
Because the LORD hath ris'n, as GOD of
　　　　Might.

The male that opes the Virgin's womb is HE ;
The Lamb of Whom His faithful people eat ;
Our truer Passover from blemish free ;
Our very GOD, Whose Name is all complete.

This yearling Lamb, our sacrifice most blest,
Our glorious Crown, for all men freely dies :
Our cleansing Pascha, beauteous from His
　　　　rest,
Behold the Sun of Righteousness arise.

Before the ark, a type to pass away,
David of old time danced : we, holier race,
Seeing the Antitype come forth to-day,
Hail with a shout, CHRIST'S own Almighty
　　　　grace.

ODE V.

ὀρθρίσωμεν ὄρθρου βαθέος.

Let us rise in early morning,
    And, instead of ointments, bring,
Hymns of praises to our Master,
    And His Resurrection sing :
We shall see the Sun of Justice
    Risen with healing on His wing.

Thy unbounded loving-kindness,
    They that groaned in Hades' chain,
Prisoners, from afar beholding,
    Hasten to the light again ;
And to that eternal Pascha
    Wove the dance and raised the strain.

Go ye forth, His Saints, to meet Him !
    Go with lamps in every hand !
From the sepulchre He riseth :
    Ready for the Bridegroom stand :
And the Pascha of salvation
    Hail, with His triumphant band.

ODE VI.

κατῆλθες ἐν τοῖς κατωτάτοις.

Into the dim earth's lowest parts descending,
 And bursting by Thy might the infernal
  chain
That bound the prisoners, Thou, at three
  days' ending
 As Jonah from the whale, hast risen again.

Thou brakest not the seal, Thy surety's
  token,
 Arising from the tomb, Who left'st in
  birth
The portals of virginity unbroken,
 And op'st the gates of heaven to sons of
  earth.

Thou, Sacrifice ineffable and living,
 Didst to the FATHER, by Thyself atone
As GOD eternal: resurrection giving
 To Adam, general parent, by Thine own.

ODE VII.

ʽΟ παῖδας ἐκ καμίνου.

Who from the fiery furnace saved the Three,
Suffers as mortal; that, His passion o'er,
This mortal, triumphing o'er death, might
be,
Vested with immortality once more.
He Whom our fathers still confest
GOD over all, for ever blest.

The women with their ointment seek the
tomb,
And Whom they mourned as dead, with
many a tear,
They worship now, joy dawning on their
gloom,
As Living GOD, as mystic Passover;
Then to the LORD'S Disciples gave
The tidings of the vanquished grave.

We keep the festal of the death of death :
Of hell o'erthrown : the first-fruits pure
and bright,

Of life eternal ; and with joyous breath
Praise Him That won the victory by His
       might :
    Him Whom our fathers still confessed
    GOD over all, for ever blest.

All hallowed festival, in splendour born !
Night of salvation and of glory !   Night
Fore-heralding the Resurrection morn !
When from the tomb the everlasting Light,
    A glorious frame once more His own,
    Upon the world in splendour shone.

ODE VIII.

αὕτη ἡ κλητή.

Thou hallowed chosen day ! that first
    And best and greatest shinest !
Lady and Queen and Feast of feasts,
    Of things divine, divinest !
On thee our praises CHRIST adore,
For ever and for evermore.

Come, let us taste the vine's new fruit
    For heavenly joy preparing :
On this propitious day, with CHRIST
    His Resurrection sharing :
Whom as True GOD our hymns adore
For ever and for evermore.

Raise, Sion, raise thine eyes ! for lo !
    Thy scattered sons have found thee :
From East and West, and North and South,
    Thy children gather round thee ;
And in thy bosom CHRIST adore,
For ever and for evermore !

O FATHER of unbounded might!
O SON and HOLY SPIRIT!
In Persons Three, in Substance One,
Of one co-equal merit;
In Thee baptiz'd, we Thee adore
For ever and for evermore!

ODE IX.

φωτίζου, φωτίζου.

Thou New Jerusalem, arise and shine!
The glory of the LORD on thee hath risen!
Sion, exult! rejoice with joy divine,
Mother of GOD! Thy Son hath burst His
    prison.

O Heavenly Voice! O word of purest love!
‘ Lo! I am with you alway to the end :’
This is the anchor, steadfast from above,
The golden anchor, whence our hopes
    depend.

O CHRIST, our Pascha! greatest, holiest,
    best!
GOD's Word and Wisdom and effectual
    Might!
Thy fuller, lovelier presence manifest,
In that eternal realm, that knows no night!

S. THOMAS'S SUNDAY.

The three following Odes are the three first of our Saint's Canon for S. Thomas's Sunday, called also Renewal Sunday : with us Low Sunday.

ODE I.

ἄσωμεν πάντες λάοι.

Come, ye faithful, raise the strain
　　Of triumphant gladness !
GOD hath brought His Israel
　　Into joy from sadness :
Loosed from Pharaoh's bitter yoke
　　Jacob's sons and daughters ;
Led them with unmoistened foot
　　Through the Red Sea waters.

'Tis the Spring of souls to-day :
　　CHRIST hath burst His prison ;
And from three days' sleep in death,
　　As a sun, hath risen.

All the winter of our sins,
   Long and dark, is flying
From His Light, to Whom we give
   Laud and praise undying.

Now the Queen of Seasons, bright
   With the Day of Splendour,
With the royal Feast of feasts,
   Comes its joy to render :
Comes to glad Jerusalem,
   Who with true affection
Welcomes, in unwearied strains,
   JESU's Resurrection.

Neither might the gates of death,
   Nor the tomb's dark portal,
Nor the watchers, nor the seal,
   Hold Thee as a mortal :
But to-day amidst the Twelve
   Thou didst stand, bestowing
That Thy peace, which evermore
   Passeth human knowing.

ODE III.

στερέωσόν με, Χριστέ.

On the rock of Thy commandments
  Fix me firmly, lest I slide :
With the glory of Thy Presence
  Cover me on every side ;
Seeing none save Thee is holy,
  GOD, for ever glorified !

New immortal out of mortal,
  New existence out of old ;
This the Cross of CHRIST accomplished,
  This the Prophets had foretold :
So that we, thus newly quickened,
  Might attain the heavenly fold.

Thou Who comprehendest all things,
  Comprehended by the tomb,
Gav'st Thy Body to the graveclothes
  And the silence and the gloom :
Till through fast-closed doors Thou camest
  Thy Disciples to illume.

Every nail-print, every buffet,·
    Thou didst freely undergo,
As Thy Resurrection's witness
    To the Twelve Thou cam'st to show :
So that what *they* saw in vision,
    Future years by faith might know.

ODE IV.

μέγα τὸ μυστήριον.

CHRIST, we turn our eyes to Thee,
And this mighty mystery !
Habakkuk exclaimed of old,
In the HOLY SPIRIT bold,
'Thou shalt come in time appointed,
For the help of Thine anointed ! '

Taste of myrrh He deign'd to know,
Who redeem'd the source of woe :
Now He bids all sickness cease
Through the honey-comb of peace :
And to this world deigns to give
That sweet fruit by which we live.

Patient LORD ! with loving eye
Thou invitest Thomas nigh ;
Showing of that Wounded Side :
While the world is certified,
How the third day, from the grave,
JESUS CHRIST arose to save.

Blest, O Didymus, the tongue
Where that first confession hung:
First the SAVIOUR to proclaim,
First the LORD of Life to name:
Such the graces it supplied,
—That dear touch of JESU's side!

THE STICHERA OF THE LAST KISS.

Δεῦτε τελευταῖον ἄσπασμον δῶμεν.

The following Stichera, which are generally, (though without any great cause,) attributed to S. John Damascene, form, perhaps, one of the most striking portions of the service of the Eastern Church. They are sung towards the conclusion of the Funeral Office, while the friends and relations are, in turns, kissing the corpse; the Priest does so last of all. Immediately afterwards, it is borne to the grave; the Priest casts the first earth on the coffin, with the words,—"The earth is the LORD's, and all that therein is: the compass of the world, and they that dwell therein." I have omitted four of the stanzas, as being almost a repetition of the rest.

Take the last kiss,—the last for ever!
   Yet render thanks amidst your gloom :
He, severed from his home and kindred,
   Is passing on towards the tomb :
For earthly labours, earthly pleasures,
   And carnal joys, he cares no more :
Where are his kinsfolk and acquaintance ?
   They stand upon another shore.
     Let us say, around him pressed,
     Grant him, LORD, eternal rest !

The hour of woe and separation,
   The hour of falling tears is this.
Him that so lately was among us
   For the last time of all we kiss :
Up to the grave to be surrendered,
   Sealed with the monumental stone,
A dweller in the house of darkness,
   Amidst the dead to lie alone.
     Let us say, around him pressed,
     Grant him, LORD, eternal rest !

Life, and life's evil conversation,
   And all its dreams, are passed away.
The soul hath left her tabernacle :
   Black and unsightly grows the clay :
The golden vessel here lies broken :
   The tongue no voice of answer knows :
Hushed is sensation, stilled is motion ;
   Toward the tomb the dead man goes.
     Let us cry with heart's endeavour,
     Grant him rest that is for ever !

What is our life ?   A fading flower ;
   A vapour, passing soon away ;
The dewdrops of the early morning :———
   Come, gaze upon the tombs to-day.
Where now is youth ?   Where now is beauty,
   And grace of form, and sparkling eye ?
All, like the summer grass, are withered ;
   All are abolished utterly !
     While our eyes with grief grow dim,
     Let us weep to CHRIST for him !

Woe for that bitter, bitter moment,
    The fearful start, the parting groan,
The wrench of anguish, from the body
    When the poor soul goes forth alone!
Hell and destructiou are before her;
    Earth in its truest worth she sees;
A flickering shade; a dream of error;
    A vanity of vanities.
        Sin in this world let us flee,
        That in heaven our place may be.

Draw nigh, ye sons of Adam; viewing
    A likeness of yourselves in clay:
Its beauty gone; its grace disfigured;
    Dissolving in the tomb's decay;
The prey of worms and of corruption,
    In silent darkness mouldering on;
Earth gathers round the coffin, hiding
    The brother, now for ever gone.
        Yet we cry, around him pressed,
        Grant him, LORD, eternal rest!

When, hurried forth by fearful angels,
  The soul forsakes her earthly frame,
Then friends and kindred she forgetteth,
  And this world's cares have no more claim,
Then passed are vanity and labour ;
  She hears the Judge's voice alone ;
She sees the ineffable tribunal :
  Where we, too, cry with suppliant moan,
    For the sins that soul hath done,
    Grant Thy pardon, Holy One !

Now all the organs of the body,
  So full of energy before,
Have lost perception, know not motion,
  Can suffer and can act no more.
The eyes are closed in death's dark shadow;
  The ear can never hear again ;
The feet are bound ; the hands lie idle ;
  The tongue is fast as with a chain.
    Great and mighty though he be,
    Every man is vanity.

Behold and weep me, friends and brethren!
  Voice, sense, and breath, and motion gone;
But yesterday I dwelt among you;
  Then death's most fearful hour came on.
Embrace me with the last embracement;
  Kiss me with this, the latest kiss;
Never again shall I be with you;
  Never with you share woe or bliss.
I go toward the dread tribunal
  Where no man's person is preferred;
Where lord and slave, where chief and soldier,
  Where rich and poor, alike are heard:
One is the manner of their judgment;
  Their plea and their condition one:
And they shall reap in woe or glory
  The earthly deeds that they have done.
I pray you, brethren, I adjure you,
  Pour forth to CHRIST the ceaseless prayer,
He would not doom me to Gehenna,
  But in His glory give me share!

IDIOMELA FOR ALL SAINTS.

——

τὰς ἕδρὰς τὰς αἰωνίας.

Those eternal bowers
   Man hath never trod,
Those unfading flowers
   Round the Throne of GOD:
Who may hope to gain them
   After weary fight?
Who at length attain them
   Clad in robes of white?——

He, who gladly barters
   All on earthly ground;
He who, like the Martyrs,
   Says, 'I WILL be crown'd:'
He, whose one oblation
   Is a life of love;
Clinging to the nation
   Of the Blest above.

Shame upon you, legions
    Of the Heavenly King,
Denizens of regions
    Past imagining!
What! with pipe and tabor
    Fool away the light,
When He bids you labour,—
    When He tells you,—'Fight!'

While I do my duty,
    Struggling through the tide,
Whisper Thou of beauty
    On the other side!
Tell who will the story
    Of our *now* distress:
Oh the future glory!
    Oh the loveliness!

S. Cosmas,

Surnamed The Melodist.

✝ A.D. 760.

S. Cosmas of Jerusalem holds the second place amidst Greek Ecclesiastical poets. Left an orphan at an early age, he was adopted by the father of S. John Damascene; and the two foster brothers were bound together by a friendship which lasted through life. They excited each other to Hymnology, and assisted, corrected, and polished each other's compositions. Cosmas, like his friend, became a monk of S. Sabbas : and against his will was consecrated Bishop of Maiuma, near Gaza, by John, Patriarch of Jerusalem ; the same who ordained Damascene Priest. After administering his diocese with great holiness, he departed this life in a good old age, about 760, and is commemorated by the Eastern Church on the 14th of October.

F 2

" Where perfect sweetness dwells, is Cosmas gone;
  But his sweet lays to cheer the Church live on,"

says the stichos prefixed to his life.

His compositions are tolerably numerous,
and he seems to have taken a pleasure in
competing with S. John Damascene, as in
the Nativity, the Epiphany, the Transfiguration, where the Canons of both are given.
To Cosmas, a considerable part of the
Octoechus is owing. The best of his compositions, besides those already mentioned,
seem to be his Canons on S. Gregory
Nazianzen, and the Purification. He is
the most learned of the Greek Church-
poets : and his fondness for types, boldness in their application, and love of
aggregating them, make him the Oriental
Adam of S. Victor. It is owing partly to a
compressed fulness of meaning, very un-
common in the Greek poets of the Church,
partly to the unusual harshness and con-
traction of his phrases, that he is the hardest
of ecclesiastical bards to comprehend.

CANON FOR CHRISTMAS DAY.

ODE I.

Χριστὸς γεννᾶται· δοξάσατε.

CHRIST is born!   Tell forth His fame!
CHRIST from Heaven! His love proclaim!
CHRIST on earth!   Exalt His Name!
Sing to the LORD, O world, with exultation!
Break forth in glad thanksgiving, every
   nation!
      For He hath triumphed gloriously!

Man, in GOD's own Image made,
Man, by Satan's wiles betrayed,
Man, on whom corruption preyed,
Shut out from hope of life and of salvation,
To-day CHRIST maketh him a new creation,
      For He hath triumphed gloriously!

For the Maker, when His foe
Wrought the creature death and woe,
Bowed the Heav'ns, and came below, (1)

And, in the Virgin's womb His dwelling
  making,
Became True Man, man's very nature
  taking;
      For He hath triumphed gloriously!

He, the Wisdom, WORD, and Might,
GOD, and SON, and Light of light,
Undiscovered by the sight
Of earthly monarch, or infernal spirit,
Incarnate was, that we might Heav'n inherit:
      For He hath triumphed gloriously!

(1.) The reference is, of course, to Psalm xviii., 9:
—" He bowed the Heavens also, and came down."

ODE III.

τῷ πρὸ τῶν αἰώνων.

Him, of the FATHER'S very Essence,
　Begotten, ere the world began,
And, in the latter time, of Mary,
　Without a human sire, made Man :
　　Unto Him, this glorious morn,
　　Be the strain outpoured ;
　　Thou That liftest up our horn,
　　Holy art Thou, LORD !

The earthly Adam, erewhile quicken'd
　By the blest breath of GOD on high,
Now made the victim of corruption,
　By woman's guile betray'd to die,
　　He, deceiv'd by woman's part ;
　　Supplication pour'd,
　　Thou Who in my nature art,
　　Holy art Thou, LORD !

Thou, JESUS CHRIST, wast consubstantial
    With this our perishable clay,
And, by assuming earthly nature,
    Exalted'st it to heavenly day.
        Thou, That wast as mortal born,
           Being GOD ador'd,
        Thou That liftest up our horn,
           Holy art Thou, LORD !

Rejoice, O Bethlehem, the city
    Whence Judah's monarchs had their birth;
Where He that sitteth on the Cherubs,
    The King of Israel, came on earth :
        Manifested this blest morn,
           As of old time never,
        He hath lifted up our horn,
           He shall reign for ever !

ODE IV.

'Ράβδος ἐκ τῆς ῥίζης.

Rod of the Root of Jesse,
 Thou, Flower of Mary born,
From that thick shady mountain (1)
 Cam'st glorious forth this morn :
Of her, the Ever Virgin,
 Incarnate wast Thou made,
The immaterial Essence,
 The GOD by all obeyed !
  Glory, LORD, Thy servants pay
  To Thy wondrous might to-day!

The Gentiles' expectation,
 Whom Jacob's words foretell,
Who Syria's pride shall vanquish,
 Samaria's power shalt quell ;
Thou from the Root of Judah
 Like some fair plant dost spring,
To turn old Gentile error
 To Thee, its GOD and King !
  Glory, LORD, Thy servants pay
  To Thy wondrous might to-day!

In Balaam's ancient vision
　　The Eastern seers were skilled;
They marked the constellations,
　　And joy their spirits filled:
For Thou, bright Star of Jacob,
　　Arising in Thy might,
Didst call these Gentile first-fruits
　　To worship in Thy light.
　　　　They, in holy reverence bent,
　　　　Gifts acceptable present.

As on a fleece descending
　　The gentle dews distil,
As drops the earth that water,
　　The Virgin didst Thou fill.
Tarshish and Ethiopia,
　　The Isles and Araby,
And Media, leagued with Sheba,
　　Fall down and worship Thee.
　　　　Glory, LORD, Thy servants pay
　　　　To Thy wondrous might to-day!

(1.) The reference is to the Song of Habakkuk:
(ili. 1), where the lxx. give—" GOD shall come from
Teman, and The Holy from the thick and shady
mountain of Paran."

ODE V.

Θεὸς ὢν εἰρήνης.

Father of Peace, and GOD of Consolation!
  The Angel of the Counsel dost Thou send
To herald peace, to manifest Salvation,
    Thy Light to pour, Thy knowledge to
      extend;
Whence, with the morning's earliest rays,
Lover of men! Thy Name wc praise.

Midst Cæsar's subjects Thou, at his decreeing,
  Obey'd'st and wast enroll'd: our mortal
    race,
To sin and Satan slave, from bondage freeing,
  Our poverty in all points didst embrace:
And by that Union didst combine
The earthly with the All-Divine.

Behold! The Virgin, prophecy sustaining,
  Incarnate Deity conceived and bore:
Virgin in birth, and Virgin still remaining:
  And man to GOD is reconciled once more:
Wherefore in faith her name we bless,
And Mother of our GOD confess.

ODE VI.

σπλάγχνων Ἰωνᾶν.

As Jonah, issuing from his three days' tomb,
  At length was cast, uninjured, on the earth;
So, from the Virgin's unpolluted womb
    The Incarnate WORD, That dwelt there,
      had His Birth:
For He, Who knew no taint of mortal stain,
Willed that His Mother spotless should
    remain.

CHRIST comes, Incarnate GOD, amongst
      us now,
  Begotten of the FATHER ere the day:
And He, to Whom the sinless legions bow,
    Lies cradled, midst unconscious beasts, on
      hay:
And, by His homely swaddling-bands girt in,
Looses the many fetters of our sin.

Now the New Child of Adam's race draws
     nigh,
  To us, the faithful, given : This, this is He
That shall the Father of Eternity,
  The Angel of the Mighty Counsel, be :
This the eternal GOD, by Whose strong hands
The fabric of the world supported stands.

ODE VII.

οἱ παῖδες εὐσεβέιᾳ.

The Holy Children boldly stand
Against the tyrant's dread command :
The kindled furnace they defy,—
No doom can shake their constancy :
They in the midmost flame confess'd,
" GOD of our Fathers !   Thou art bless'd !"

The Shepherds keep their flocks by night ;
The Heav'n glows out with wond'rous light;
The glory of the LORD is there,
The Angel-bands their King declare :
The watchers of the night confess'd,
" GOD of our Fathers !   Thou art bless'd !"

The Angel ceas'd ; and suddenly
Seraphic legions fill'd the sky :
Glory to GOD, they cry again :
Peace upon earth, good will to men :
CHRIST comes !—And they that heard
            confess'd,
" GOD of our Fathers !   Thou art bless'd !"

What said the Shepherds ?—Let us turn
This new-born miracle to learn.
To Bethlehem's gate their footsteps drew :
The Mother with the Child they view :
They knelt, and worshipp'd, and confess'd,
" GOD of our Fathers !   Thou art bless'd !"

ODE VIII.

θαύματος ὑπερφυοῦς ἡ δροσοβόλος.

The dewy freshness that the furnace flings
Works out a wond'rous type of future things:
Nor did the flame the Holy Three consume,
Nor did the Godhead's fire thy frame entomb,
    Thou, on Whose bosom hung the WORD:
      Wherefore we cry with heart's endeavour,
    " Let all Creation bless the LORD,
      And magnify His Name for ever!"

Babel's proud daughter once led David's
      race
From Sion, to their exile's woeful place:
She bids her wise men now, with gifts in
      hand,
Before King David's Royal Daughter stand,
    The Mother of the Incarnate WORD:
      Wherefore we cry with heart's endeavour,
    " Let all Creation bless the LORD,
      And magnify His Name for ever!"

From music grief held back the exiles' hand:
"How sing the LORD's song in an alien
    land?"
But Babel's exile here is done away,
And Bethlehem's harmony this glorious day
    By Thee, Incarnate GOD, restored:
        Wherefore we cry with heart's endeavour,
    "Let all Creation bless the LORD,
        And magnify His Name for ever!"

Of old victorious Babel bore away
The spoils of Royal Sion and her prey:
But Babel's treasure now, and Babel's kings,
CHRIST, by the guiding star, to Sion brings.
    There have they knelt, and there ador'd:
        Wherefore we cry with heart's endeavour,
    " Let all Creation bless the LORD,
        And magnify His Name for ever!"

G

ODE IX.

μυστήριον ξένον.

O wond'rous mystery, full of passing grace !
  The grot becometh Heav'n : the Virgin's
        breast
The bright Cherubic Throne : the stall that
        place,
    Where He, Who fills all space, vouchsafes
        to rest :
      CHRIST our GOD, to Whom we raise
      Hymns of thankfulness and praise !

The course propitious of the unknown Star
  The Magi follow'd on its heav'nly way,—
Until it led them, beckoning from afar,
    To where the CHRIST, the King of all
        things, lay :
      Him in Bethlehem they find,
      Born the SAVIOUR of mankind.

" Where is the Child," they ask, "the new-
　　born King,
　Whose herald-light is glittering in the
　　sky,—
To Whom our offerings and our praise we
　　bring?"
　And Herod's heart is troubled utterly.
　　Armed for war with GOD, in vain
　　Would he see that Infant slain.

TRANSFIGURATION.

———

I shall, perhaps, make the following Canon more acceptable to most readers, if, instead of translating the Odes in detail, I make a cento from the more remarkable Troparia.

They are principally from the first four Odes.

χορὸς ᾽Ισραήλ.

The choirs of ransomed Israel,
  The Red Sea's passage o'er,
Uprais'd the hymn of triumph
  Upon the further shore :
And shouted, as the foeman
  Was whelm'd beneath the sea,—
' Sing we to Judah's Saviour,
  For glorified is He !'

Amongst His Twelve Apostles
  CHRIST spake the Words of Life,
And shew'd a realm of beauty
  Beyond a world of strife :

' When all My FATHER's glory
   Shall shine express'd in Me,
Then praise Him, then exalt Him,
   For magnified is He!'

Upon the Mount of Tabor
   The promise was made good;
When, baring all the Godhead,
   In light itself He stood:
And they, in awe beholding,
   The Apostolic Three,
Sang out to GOD their Saviour,
   For magnified was He!

In days of old, on Sinai,
   The LORD Jehovah came,
In majesty of terror,
   In thunder-cloud and flame:
On Tabor, with the glory
   Of sunniest light for vest,
The excellence of beauty
   In JESUS was express'd.

All hours and days inclin'd there,
   And did Thee worship meet;
The sun himself adored Thee,
   And bow'd him at Thy feet:

While Moses and Elias
   Upon the Holy Mount,
The co-eternal glory
   Of CHRIST our GOD recount.

O holy, wond'rous Vision!
   But what, when this life past,
The beauty of Mount Tabor
   Shall end in Heav'n at last?
But what, when all the glory
   Of uncreated light
Shall be the promis'd guerdon
   Of them that win the fight?

S. Stephen the Sabaite.
A.D. 725........A.D. 794.

S. Stephen, called the Sabaïte, from the monastery of S. Sabbas, was the nephew of S. John Damascene, who placed him in that house. He was then ten years of age : he passed fifty-nine years in that retreat; and was the earliest of the hymnographers who lived to see the final restoration of Icons. He has left but few poetical compositions. The two best are those on the Martyrs of the monastery of S. Sabbas—(March 20)—on which a monk of that house would be likely to write *con amore;* and on the Circumcision. His style seems formed on that of S. Cosmas, rather than that of his own uncle. He is not deficient in elegance and richness of typology, but exhibits much of sameness, and is occasionally full of very hard metaphors, as when he speaks of "the circumcision of the tempest of our souls." He is commemorated on the 13th of July.

IDIOMELA IN THE WEEK OF THE FIRST OBLIQUE TONE.

———

These Stanzas, which strike me as very sweet, are
not in all the editions of the Octoechus. I copy
from a dateless Constantinopolitan book.

κόπον τε καὶ κάματον.

Art thou weary, art thou languid,
  Art thou sore distrest?
" Come to Me"—saith One—"and coming,
    Be at rest !"

Hath He marks to lead me to Him,
  If He be my Guide?
" In His Feet and Hands are Wound-prints,
    And His Side."

Is there Diadem, as Monarch,
  That His Brow adorns?
" Yea, a Crown, in very surety,
    But of Thorns !"

If I find Him, if I follow,
  What His guerdon here ?
" Many a sorrow, many a labour,
        Many a tear."

If I still hold closely to Him,
  What hath He at last ?
" Sorrow vanquish'd, labour ended,
        Jordan past ! "

If I ask Him to receive me,
  Will He say me nay ?
" Not till earth, and not till heaven
        Pass away ! "

Finding, following, keeping, struggling,
  Is He sure to bless ?
" Angels, Martyrs, Prophets, Virgins,
        Answer, Yes ! "

S. Tarasius.

+ A.D. 806.

Tarasius, raised by Constantine and Irene from the post of Secretary of State, at one step, though a layman, to the Patriarchate of Constantinople, (784 A.D.) was the chief mover in the restoration of Icons and the Second Council of Nicæa. Strongly opposing the divorce of Constantine from Maria, he refused to celebrate that Emperor's nuptials with Theodora. But when they had been performed, he was with some difficulty persuaded to pardon the priest who had officiated at them. On this, S. Plato, and the monks of the all-influential Studium, forsook his communion; nor was the schism composed till the Patriarch yielded and retracted his pardon. He died

February 25, A.D. 806, on which day he is commemorated both by the East and West. His hymns are unimportant. The longest is the Canon on the Invention of S. John Baptist, May 25. It is in no wise remarkable. Nor do I know any of his compositions which would be sufficiently interesting to the English reader, to make it worth versification here.

S. Theophanes.

A.D. 759......A.D. 818.

———

S. Theophanes, who holds the third place among Greek poets, was born in 759, his father being Governor of the Archipelago. Betrothed in childhood to a lady named Megalis, he persuaded her, on their wedding-day, to embrace the monastic life. He retired to the monastery of Syngriana, in the early part of the reign of Constantine and Irene. From the fiftieth year of his age he was nearly bedridden; but his devotion to the cause of Icons marked him out as one of the earliest victims of Leo the Armenian, who, after imprisoning him for two years, banished him to Samothrace. On the third day after his arrival in that inhospitable region, worn out with sufferings and sickness, he departed this life A.D.

818. He is chiefly famous for his History, with which we have now nothing to do. With the one exception of S. Joseph of the Studium, Theophanes is the most prolific of Eastern Hymnographers; and in his writings we first see that which has been the bane and ruin of later Greek poetry, the composition of hymns, not from the spontaneous effusion of the heart, but because they were wanted to fill up a gap in the Office-Book.

Because the great festivals and the chief Saints of the Church had their Canon and their Stichera, therefore every martyr, every confessor, who happened to give his name to a day, must have his Canon and Stichera also, just for uniformity. How different the Latin use, where not even the Apostles have separate hymns, received by the whole Church, but supply themselves from the *Common!* Hence the deluge of worthless compositions that occur in the Menæa: hence tautology, repeated till it becomes almost sickening; the merest commonplace,

again and again decked in the tawdry shreds
of tragic language, and twenty or thirty
times presenting the same thought in
slightly varying terms. Theophanes, indeed, must be distinguished from the host
of inferior writers that about his time began
to overwhelm the Church. Many of his
subjects are of world-wide interest. The
Eastern martyrs whom he celebrates, are,
for the most part, those who have won for
themselves the greatest name in the annals
of history. But still we find him thus
honoring some, of whom all that can be
said is, that they died for the Name of
CHRIST. And though the poet brings
more matter to his task than do others,
many long stanzas, that keep pretty close
to their subject, concerning a Saint of whom
there is nothing especial to say, must become
tedious.

IDIOMELA
ON FRIDAY OF TYROPHAGUS,
THAT IS,
OF QUINQUAGESIMA.

At this period of the year the weeks are named, not from the Sundays that precede, but from those that follow, them. Quinquagesima is termed Tyrophagus, because up to that time, but not beyond, cheese is allowed. The Friday previous is appropriated to the Commemoration of All Holy Ascetes; in order, as the Synaxarion says, that, by the remembrance of their conflict, we may be invigorated for the race that is set before us.

Δεῦτε ἅπαντες πιστοί.

Hither, and with one accord,
Sing the servants of the LORD :
Sing each great ascetic sire ;—
Anthony shall lead the choir :
Let Euthymius next him stand ;
Then, in order, all the band.
Make we joyous celebration
Of their heavenly conversation ;

Of their glory, how they rise,
Like another Paradise :
These the trees our GOD hath plac'd,
Trees, with fruit immortal grac'd ;
Bringing forth, for CHRIST on high,
Flowers of Life that cannot die ;
With the sweetness that they fling
Mortal spirits nourishing.

 Filled with GOD, and ever blest,
 For our pardon make request !

Egypt, hail, thou faithful strand !
Hail, thou holy Libyan land !
Nurturing for the realm on high
Such a glorious company !
They by many a toil intense,
Chastity and continence,
Perfect men to GOD upreared,
Stars to guide us have appeared :
They, by many a glorious sign,
Many a beam of Power Divine,
To the earth's remotest shore
Far and wide their radiance pour.

 Holy Fathers, bright and blest,
 For our pardon make request !

By what skill of mortal tongue
Shall your wondrous acts be sung ?
All the conflicts of the soul,
All your struggles towards the goal ;
And your virtues' prize immense,
And your victories over sense,
How perpetual watch ye kept
Over passion, prayed and wept :
Yea, like very angels came,
Visible in earthly frame,
And with Satan girt for fight
Utterly o'erthrew his might.
Fam'd for signs and wonders rare,
Join to ours, great Saints, your prayer :
    Ask that we, ye ever blest,
    May attain the Land of Rest !

STICHERA AT THE FIRST VESPERS
OF CHEESE SUNDAY.
(Quinquagesima.)

ADAM'S COMPLAINT.

The reader can hardly fail to be struck with the
beautiful idea in the third stanza, where the foliage
of Paradise is asked to make intercession for Adam's
recall. The last stanza, Milton, as an universal
scholar, doubtless had in his eye, in Eve's lament-
ation.

" The LORD my Maker, forming me of clay,
By His own Breath the breath of life convey'd:
O'er all the bright new world He gave me
          sway,—
A little lower than the Angels made.
But Satan, using for his guile
The crafty serpent's cruel wile,
Deceiv'd me by the Tree ;
And severed me from GOD and grace,
And wrought me death, and all my race,
As long as time shall be.
O Lover of the sons of men !
Forgive, and call me back again !

"In that same hour I lost the glorious stole
Of innocence, that GOD's own Hands had
     made;
And now the tempter poisoning all my soul,
I sit, in fig leaves and in skins arrayed :
I sit condemn'd, distress'd, forsaken ;
Must till the ground whence I was taken
By labour's daily sweat.
But Thou, That shalt hereafter come,
The Offspring of a Virgin-womb,
Have pity on me yet !
O turn on me those gracious eyes,
And call me back to Paradise !

"O glorious Paradise !   O lovely clime !
O God-built mansions ! Joy of every Saint !
Happy remembrance to all coming time !
Whisper, with all thy leaves, in cadence
     faint,
One prayer to Him Who made them all,
One prayer for Adam in his fall !—
That He, Who formed thy gates of yore,
Would bid those gates unfold once more
That I had closed by sin :

And let me taste that holy Tree
That giveth immortality
To them that dwell therein !
Or have I fallen so far from grace
That mercy hath for me no place ?"

Adam sat right against the Eastern gate,
By many a storm of sad remembrance tost :
"O me! so ruined by the serpent's hate!
O me! so glorious once, and now so lost!
So mad that bitter lot to choose!
Beguil'd of all I had to lose!
Must I then, gladness of my eyes,—
Must I then leave thee, Paradise,
And as an exile go ?
And must I never cease to grieve
How once my GOD, at cool of eve,
Came down to walk below?
O Merciful! on Thee I call :
O Pitiful! forgive my Fall !"

S. Theodore of the Studium.

✝ 826.

Theodore of the Studium, by his sufferings and his influence, did more, perhaps, in the cause of Icons than any other man. His uncle, S. Plato, and himself, had been cruelly persecuted by Constantine for refusing to communicate with him after his illicit marriage with Theodota, at a time when, as we have seen, the firmness of even the Patriarch Tarasius gave way. Raised subsequently to be Hegumen of the great abbey of the Studium, the first at Constantinople, and probably the most influential that ever existed in the world, Theodore exhibited more doubtful conduct in the schism which regarded the readmission to communion of Joseph, the priest who had given the nuptial benediction to Constantine: but he suffered imprisonment on this account with the greatest firmness. When the Iconoclastic persecution again broke out under Leo the Armenian, Theodore was one of the first sufferers : he was exiled, imprisoned, scourged, and left for dead. Under Michael Curopalata he enjoyed greater liberty ; but he died in banishment, Nov. 11, A.D. 826. His hymns are, in my judgment, very far superior to those of S. Theophanes,—and nearly, if not quite, equal to the works of S. Cosmas. In those (comparatively few) which he has left for the Festivals of Saints, he does not appear to advantage : it is in his Lent Canons, in the Triodion, that his great excellency lies. The contrast there presented between the rigid, unbending, unyielding character of the man in his outward history, and the fervent gush of penitence and love which his inward life, as revealed by these compositions, manifests, is very striking ;—it forms a remarkable parallel to the characters of S. Gregory VII., Innocent III., and other holy men of the

Western Church, whom the world, judging
from a superficial view of their characters,
has branded with unbending haughtiness,
and the merest formality in religion, while
their most secret writings show them to have
been clinging to the Cross in an ecstasy of
love and sorrow.

CANON FOR APOCREOS.

Apocreos is our Sexagesima, and is so
called, because meat is not eaten beyond it.
The Synaxarion, (which will explain the
following poem), begins thus:

"On this day, we commemorate
the Second and impartial Coming
of our Lord Jesus Christ.

Stichos. When He, the Judge of all things,
   sits to doom,
    Oh grant that I may hear His joyful
    ' *Come !'*

This commemoration the most Divine
Fathers set after the two parables," (*i.e.*,
the Gospels of the two preceding Sundays,
The Pharisee and Publican, and the Prodigal
Son,) "lest any one, learning from them the
mercy of God, should live carelessly, and

say, ' GOD is merciful, and whenever I wish to relinquish sin, it will be in my power to accomplish my purpose.' They therefore here commemorated that fearful day, that, by the consideration of death, and the expectation of the dreadful things that shall hereafter be, they might terrify men of negligent life, and bring them back again to virtue, and might teach them not simply to put confidence in GOD's mercy, considered by itself, but to remember also that the Judge is just, and will render to every man according to his works." As the Eastern Church has no such season as Advent, this commemoration becomes more peculiarly appropriate.

The Canon that follows is unfortunate in provoking a comparison with the unapproachable majesty of the *Dies Iræ*. Yet during the four hundred years which it anticipated that sequence, it was undoubtedly the grandest Judgment-hymn of the Church. Its faults are those of most of the class : it eddies round and round the subject, without making way,—its different portions have no very great connection with each other,—and its great length is accompanied by considerable tautology. Yet, in spite of these defects, it is impossible to deny that the great common-places of Death and Judgment are very nobly set forth in this poem. On account of its length, I give the first three and last Odes only.

ODE I.

τὴν ἡμέραν τὴν φρικτήν.

That fearful day, that day of speechless dread,
When Thou shalt come to judge the quick
and dead——
  I shudder to foresee,
  O GOD! what then shall be!

When Thou shalt come, angelic legions
 round,
With thousand thousands, and with trumpet
 sound;
  CHRIST, grant me in the air
  With saints to meet Thee there!

Weep, O my soul, ere that great hour and day,
When GOD shall shine in manifest array,
  Thy sin, that thou may'st be
  In that strict judgment free!

The terror !—hell-fire fierce and unsufficed :
The bitter worm : the gnashing teeth :—O
    CHRIST,
        Forgive, remit, protect ;
        And set me with the elect !

That I may hear the blessed voice that calls
The righteous to the joy of heavenly halls :
        And, King of Heaven, may reach
        The realm that passeth speech !

Enter Thou not in judgment with each deed,
Nor each intent and thought in strictness
    read :
        Forgive, and save me then,
        O Thou That lovest men !

Thee, One in Three blest Persons ! LORD
    o'er all !
Essence of essence, Power of power, we call :
        Save us, O FATHER, SON,
        And SPIRIT, ever one !

ODE III.

'Ο Κύριος ἔρχεται.

God comes;—and who shall stand before
    His fear ?
Who bide His Presence, when He draweth
    near ?
        My soul, my soul, prepare
        To kneel before Him there !

Haste,—weep,—be reconciled to Him before
The fearful judgment knocketh at the door :
        Where, in the Judge's eyes,
        All bare and naked lies.

Have mercy, Lord, have mercy, Lord, I
    cry,
When with Thine angels Thou appear'st on
    high :
        And man a doom inherits,
        According to his merits.

How can I bear Thy fearful anger, LORD ?
I, that so often have transgressed Thy word?
    But put my sins away,
    And spare me in that day !

O miserable soul, return, lament,
Ere earthly converse end, and life be spent:
    Ere, time for sorrow o'er,
    The Bridegroom close the door !

Yea, I have sinned, as no man sinned beside:
With more than human guilt my soul is
    dyed :
    But spare, and save me here,
    Before that day appear !

Three Persons in One Essence uncreate,
On Whom, both Three and One, our praises
    wait,
    Give everlasting light
    To them that sing Thy might !

ODE IV.

ἐφέστηκεν ἡ ἡμέρα.

The Day is near, the Judgment is at hand,
Awake, my soul, awake, and ready stand!
Where chiefs shall go with them that filled
    the throne,
Where rich and poor the same tribunal own;
        And every thought and deed
        Shall find its righteous meed.

There with the sheep the shepherd of the fold
Shall stand together; there the young and
    old;
Master and slave one doom shall undergo;
Widow and maiden one tribunal know.
        Oh woe, oh woe, to them
        Whom lawless lives condemn!

That Judgment-seat, impartial in decree,
Accepts no bribe, admits no subtilty:
No orator persuasion may exert,
No perjured witness wrong to right convert:
        But all things, hid in night,
        Shall then be dragged to light.

Let me not enter in the land of woe;
Let me not realms of outer darkness know!
Nor from the wedding-feast reject Thou me,
For my soiled vest of immortality;
   Bound hand and foot, and cast
   In anguish that shall last!

When Thou, the nations ranged on either
  side,
The righteous from the sinners shalt divide,
Then give me to be found amongst Thy
  sheep,
Then from the goats Thy trembling servant
  keep:
   That I may hear the voice
   That bids Thy Saints rejoice!

When righteous inquisition shall be made,
And the books opened, and the thrones
  arrayed,
My soul, what plea to shield thee canst thou
  know,
Who hast no fruit of righteousness to show,
   No holy deeds to bring
   To CHRIST the LORD and King?

I hear the rich man's wail and bitter cry,
Out of the torments of eternity;
I know, beholding that devouring flame,
My guilt and condemnation are the same;
  And spare me, LORD, I say,
  In the great Judgment Day!

The WORD and SPIRIT, with the FATHER
  One,
One Light and emanation of One Sun,
The WORD by generation, we adore,
The SPIRIT by procession, evermore;
  And with creation raise
  The thankful hymn of praise.

ODE IX.

῾Ο Κύριος ἔρχεται.

The LORD draws nigh, the righteous Throne's
    Assessor,
The just to save, to punish the Transgressor:
      Weep we, and mourn, and pray,
      Regardful of that day;
When all the secrets of all hearts shall be
Lit with the blaze of full eternity.

Clouds and thick darkness o'er the Mount
    assembling,
Moses beheld the Eternal's glory, trembling :
      And yet he might but see
      GOD's feebler Majesty.
And I—I needs must view His fullest
    Face :—
O spare me, LORD ! O take me to Thy
    grace !

David of old beheld, in speechless terror,
The session of the Judge—the doom of
    error :
      And what have I to plead
      For mercy in my need ?
Nothing save this : O grant me yet to be,
Ere that day come, renewed and true to Thee !

Here, fires of deep damnation roar and
    glitter :
The worm is deathless, and the cup is bitter :
      There, day that hath no morrow,
      And joy that hath no sorrow :
And who so blest that he shall fly the abyss,
Rais'd up to God's Right Hand, and speech-
    less bliss !

My soul with many an act of sin is wounded :
With mortal weakness is my frame sur-
    rounded :
      My life is well nigh o'er :
      The Judge is at the door :
How wilt thou, miserable spirit, fare,
What time He sends His summons through
    the air ?

ORTHODOXY SUNDAY.

The first Sunday in Lent is kept in memory; primarily, of the final triumph of the Church over the Iconoclasts in 842; and, incidentally, of her victory over all other heresies. It has a kind of commination appropriate to itself alone. The following Canon is ascribed to S. Theodore of the Studium, though Baronius has thought that it cannot be his, because it implies that peace was restored to the Church, whereas that hymnographer died while the persecution still continued. Very possibly, however, it was written on the temporary victory of the Church, which did occur in the time of S. Theodore; and then, in 842, may have been lengthened and adapted to the then state of things, perhaps by Naucratius, the favorite disciple of S. Theodore. It is, perhaps, the most spirited of all the Canons,

though many of its expressions savour too
much of bitterness and personal feeling to
be well defended, and the reader must con-
stantly bear in mind that the poet feels the
cause, not so much of Icons, as of the
Incarnation itself, to be at stake. I have
only given about one-third of the poem.
The stanzas are these : Ode I. Tropar. 1, 2 ;
III. 6 ; IV. 1, 2, 3 ; V. 1, 3, 4, 5 ; VI. 1 ;
IX. 2, 3, 4, 5.

Χαριστήριον ᾠδήν.

A song, a song of gladness !
  A song of thanks and praise !
The horn of our salvation
  Hath GOD vouchsafed to raise !
A monarch, true and faithful,
  And glorious in her might,
To champion CHRIST'S own quarrel,
  And Orthodoxy's right !

Now manifest is glory :
  Now grace and virtue shine :
Now joys the Church regaining
  Her ornaments divine :

And girds them on in gladness
　Of meet and fair array,
After long months of struggle,
　Long years of disarray.

Now cries the blood for vengeance,
　By persecutors poured,
Of them that died defending
　The likeness of the LORD :
The likeness, as a mortal
　That He vouchsaf'd to take,
Long years ago, in Bethlem,
　Incarnate for our sake.

Awake, O Church, and triumph !
　Exult, each realm and land !
And open let the houses,
　The ascetic houses stand !
And let the holy virgins
　With joy and song take in
Their relics and their icons,
　Who died this day to win !

Assemble ye together
 So joyous and so bold,
The ascetic troops, and pen them
 Once more within the fold!
If strength again he gather,*
 Again the foe shall fall :
If counsel he shall counsel,
 Our GOD shall scatter all.

The LORD, the LORD hath triumph'd!
 Let all the world rejoice !
Hush'd is the turmoil, silent
 His servants' tearful voice :
And the One Faith, the True Faith,
 Goes forth from East to West,
Enfolding, in its beauty,
 The earth as with a vest.

* This is from the magnificent Emmanuel Ode sung at Great Compline on high festivals.

"Having become mighty, ye have been subdued,
 "*For God is with us.*

"And if ye shall again become mighty, again
 ye shall be subdued,
  "*For God is with us.*

"And if ye shall devise any device, the
 LORD shall scatter it,
  "*For God is with us.*"

They rise, the sleepless watchmen
　　Upon the Church's wall;
With yearning supplication
　　On GOD the LORD they call:
And He, though long time silent,
　　Bow'd down a gracious ear,
His people's earnest crying
　　And long complaint to hear.

Sing, sing for joy each desert!
　　Exult, each realm of earth!
Ye mountains, drop down sweetness!
　　Ye hillocks, leap for mirth!
For CHRIST the WORD, bestowing
　　His blessed peace on men,
In Faith's most holy union
　　Hath knit His Church again.

The GOD of vengeance rises:
　　And CHRIST attacks the foe,
And makes His servants mighty
　　The wicked to o'erthrow:

And now Thy condescension
   In boldness may we hymn,
And now in peace and safety
   Thy sacred Image limn.

O LORD of loving kindness,
   How wondrous are Thy ways!
What tongue of man suffices
   Thy gentleness to praise?
Because of Thy dear Image
   Men dared Thy Saints to kill,
Yet didst Thou not consume them,
   But bar'st their insults still.

Thou who hast fixed unshaken
   Thy Church's mighty frame,
So that hell-gates shall never
   Prevail against the same;—
Bestow upon Thy people
   Thy peace, that we may bring
One voice, one hymn, one spirit,
   To glorify our King!

S. Methodius I.

† A.D. 846.

S. Methodius I., a native of Syracuse,
embraced the monastic life at Constantinople. Sent as legate from Pope Paschal to
Michael the Stammerer, he was imprisoned
by that prince in a close cell, and there
passed nine years, on account of his resolute
defence of Icons. Having been scourged
for the same cause, by the Emperor Theophilus, he made his escape from prison;
and when peace was restored to the Church
was raised to the throne of Constantinople.
His first care was to assemble a Synod for
the restoration of Icons; and it is, properly
speaking, *that* Synod which the Greeks
celebrate on Orthodoxy Sunday. With this

Council the Iconoclast troubles ceased. S.
Methodius died November 4, 846. His
compositions are very few, and are chiefly
confined to Idiomela.

That which follows seems to me the
prettiest. It is for a Sunday of the Fourth
Tone.

εἰ καὶ τὰ παρόντα.

Are thy toils and woes increasing?
Are the Foe's attacks unceasing?
    Look with Faith unclouded,
    Gaze with eyes unshrouded,
      On the Cross!

Dost thou fear that strictest trial?
Tremblest thou at CHRIST'S denial?
    Never rest without it,
    Clasp thine arms about it,
      —That dear Cross!

Diabolic legions press thee?
Thoughts and works of sin distress thee?
    It shall chase all terror,
    It shall right all error,
      That sweet Cross!

Draw'st thou nigh to Jordan's river?
Should'st thou tremble? Need'st thou
  quiver?
      No! if by it lying,—
      No! if on it dying,—
          On the Cross!

Say then,—Master, while I cherish
That sweet hope, I cannot perish!
      After this life's story,
      Give Thou me the glory
          For the Cross!

S. Joseph of the Studium.

———

The *third period* of Greek Hymnology opens with its most voluminous writer, S. Joseph of the Studium. A Sicilian by birth, he left his native country on its occupation by the Mahometans in 830, and went to Thessalonica, where he embraced the monastic life.   Thence he removed to Constantinople, but, in the second Iconoclastic persecution, he seems to have felt no vocation for confessorship, and went to Rome. Taken by pirates, he was for some years a slave in Crete, where he converted many to the faith ; and having obtained his liberty, and returned to the Imperial City, he stood high in the favour, first of S. Ignatius, then of Photius, whom he accompanied into exile.

On the death of that great man he was
recalled, and gave himself up entirely to
Hymnology.   A legend, connected with his
death, is sometimes represented on the walls
of the churches in the Levant.   A citizen
of Constantinople betook himself to the
church of S. Theodore in the hope of obtain-
ing some benefit from the intercessions of
that martyr.   He waited three days in vain;
then, just as he was about to leave the
church in despair, S. Theodore appeared.
"I," said the vision, "and the other Saints,
whom the poet Joseph has celebrated in
his Canons, have been attending his soul
to Paradise: hence my absence from my
church."   The Eastern Communion celebrates him on the 3rd of April.   But of the
innumerable compositions of this most
laborious writer it would be impossible to
find one which, to Western taste, gives the
least sanction to the position which he holds
in the East.   The insufferable tediousness
consequent on the necessity of filling eight
Odes with the praises of a Saint of whom

nothing, beyond the fact of his existence, is
known, and doing this sixty or seventy different times,—the verbiage, the bombast,
the trappings with which Scriptural simplicity is *elevated* to the taste of a corrupt
Court, are each and all scarcely to be
paralleled. He is by far the most prolific of
the hymn writers.

SUNDAY OF THE PRODIGAL SON.

(SEPTUAGESIMA.)

———

The Sunday before Septuagesima, and Septuagesima itself once, respectively, in the Greek Church, the Sunday of the Pharisee and Publican,—and the Sunday of the Prodigal Son,—those parables forming the gospel for the day, and serving for the keynote to the offices. The following Troparia are from the Canon at Lauds on Septuagesima. (Ode VI. and Ode VIII. Trop. 2, 3.

βυθὸς ἁμαρτημάτων.

The abyss of many a former sin
Encloses me, and bars me in :
Like billows my transgressions roll :
Be Thou the Pilot of my soul :
And to Salvation's harbour bring,
Thou Saviour and Thou glorious King !

My Father's heritage abused,
Wasted by lust, by sin misused ;
To shame and want and misery brought
The slave to many a fruitless thought,
I cry to Thee, Who lovest men,
O pity and receive again !

In hunger now,—no more possessed
Of that my portion bright and blest,
The exile and the alien see
Who yet would fain return to Thee !
And save me, LORD, who seek to raise
To Thy dear love the hymn of praise!

With that blest thief my prayer I make,
Remember for Thy mercy's sake!
With that poor publican I cry,
Be merciful, O GOD most High!
With that lost Prodigal I fain
Back to my home would turn again !

Mourn, mourn, my soul, with earnest care,
And raise to CHRIST the contrite prayer:—
O Thou, Who freely wast made poor,
My sorrows and my sins to cure,
Me, poor of all good works, embrace,
Enriching with Thy boundless grace !

K

THE PILGRIMS OF JESUS.

This is merely a Cento from the Canon on S S.
Chrysanthus and Daria (March 19.)

O happy band of pilgrims,
  If onward ye will tread
With JESUS as your Fellow
  To JESUS as your Head !

O happy, if ye labour
  As JESUS did for men :
O happy, if ye hunger
  As JESUS hunger'd then !

The Cross that JESUS carried
  He carried as your due :
The Crown that JESUS weareth
  He weareth it for you.

The Faith by which ye see Him,
  The Hope, in which ye yearn,
The Love that through all troubles
  To Him alone will turn,—

What are they, but vaunt-couriers
 To lead you to His Sight?
What are they, save the effluence
 Of Uncreated Light?

The trials that beset you,
 The sorrows ye endure,
The manifold temptations
 That Death alone can cure,—

What are they, but His jewels
 Of right celestial worth?
What are they but the ladder
 Set up to Heav'n on earth?

O happy band of pilgrims,
 Look upward to the skies;—
Where such a light affliction
 Shall win you such a prize!

THE RETURN HOME.

A Cento from the Canon of S. John Climacos.

Safe home, safe home in port!
—Rent cordage, shattered deck,
Torn sails, provisions short,
And only not a wreck :
But oh! the joy upon the shore,
To tell our voyage-perils o'er !

The prize, the prize secure !
The athlete nearly fell ;
Bare all he *could* endure,
And bare not always well :
But he may smile at troubles gone
Who sets the victor-garland on !

No more the foe can harm :
No more of leagur'd camp,
And cry of night-alarm,
And need of ready lamp :
And yet how nearly he had failed,—
How nearly had that foe prevailed !

The lamb is in the fold
In perfect safety penn'd :
The lion once had hold,
And thought to make an end ;
But One came by with Wounded Side,
And for the sheep the Shepherd died.

The exile is at home !
—O nights and days of tears,
O longings not to roam,
O sins, and doubts, and fears,—
What matter now, when (so men say)
The King has wip'd those tears away ?

O happy, happy Bride!
Thy widow'd hours are past,
The Bridegroom at thy side,
Thou all His Own at last !
The sorrows of thy former cup
In full fruition swallow'd up !

LET OUR CHOIR NEW ANTHEMS RAISE.

A Cento from the Canon for SS. Timothy and Maura ; May 3.

τῶν ἱερῶν ἀθλοφόρων.

Let our Choir new anthems raise :
    Wake the morn with gladness :
GOD Himself to joy and praise
    Turns the Martyrs' sadness :
This the day that won their crown,
    Opened Heav'n's bright portal ;
As they laid the mortal down,
    And put on th' immortal.

Never flinch'd they from the flame,
    From the torture, never ;
Vain the foeman's sharpest aim,
    Satan's best endeavour :
For by faith they saw the Land
    Decked in all its glory,
Where triumphant now they stand
    With the victor's story.

Faith they had that knew not shame,
   Love that could not languish;
And eternal Hope o'ercame
   Momentary anguish.
He Who trod the self-same road,
   Death and Hell defeated;
Wherefore these their passions show'd
   Calvary repeated.

Up and follow, Christian men!
   Press through toil and sorrow!
Spurn the night of fear, and then,—
   Oh the glorious morrow!
Who will venture on the strife?
   Blest who first begin it!
Who will grasp the Land of Life?
   Warriors! up and win it!

"AND WILT THOU PARDON, LORD."

The following Stanzas are a Cento from the Canon for the Monday of the First Tone; in the Paracletice.

τῶν ʽαμαρτιῶν μου τὴν πληθύν.

And wilt Thou pardon, LORD,
    A sinner such as I ?
Although Thy book his crimes record
    Of such a crimson dye ?

So deep are they engrav'd,—
    So terrible their fear,—
The righteous scarcely shall be sav'd,
    And where shall I appear ?

My soul, make all things known
    To Him Who all things sees :
That so the LAMB may yet atone
    Foa thine iniquities.

O Thou, Physician blest,
　　Make clean my guilty soul!
And me, by many a sin oppress'd,
　　Restore and keep me whole!

I know not how to praise
　　Thy mercy and Thy love:
But deign Thy servant to upraise,
　　And I shall learn above!

STARS OF THE MORNING.

A Cento from the Canon of the " Bodiless Ones."
Tuesday in the Week of the Fourth Tone.

Stars of the morning,
    Gloriously bright,
Fill'd with celestial
    Virtue and light,
These that, where night never
    Followeth day,
Raise the Trishagion
    Ever and aye :

These are Thy counsellors :
    These dost Thou own,
LORD GOD of Sabaoth !
    Nearest Thy throne ;
These are Thy ministers,
    These dost Thou send,
Help of the helpless ones !
    Man to defend.

These keep the guard, amidst
  Salem's dear bowers :
Thrones, Dominations,
  Virtues and Powers :
Where with the Living Ones,
  Mystical Four,
Cherubin, Seraphim,
  Bow and adore.

"Who like the LORD?"—thunders
  Michael, the Chief :
Raphael, "the Cure of GOD,"
  Comforteth grief :
And, as at Nazareth,
  Prophet of peace,
Gabriel, "the light of GOD,"
  Bringeth release.

Then, when the earth was first
  Pois'd in mid space,—
Then, when the planets first
  Sped on their race,—
Then, when were ended the
  Six days' employ,—
Then all the Sons of GOD
  Shouted for joy.

Still let them succour us ;
    Still let them fight,
Lord of angelic hosts,
    Battling for right !
Till, where their anthems they
    Ceaselessly pour,
We with the Angels may,
    Bow and adore !

CANON FOR ASCENSION.

This is the crowning glory of the poet Joseph: he has here with a happy boldness entered into the lists with S. John Damascene, to whom, on this one occasion, he must be pronounced superior.   I have preserved the alphabetic arrangement.   All the Catavasias are in Iambics.

ODE I.

ἀνέστης τριήμερος.

A   fter three days Thou didst rise
    Visible to mortal eyes :
    First the Eleven worshipped Thee,—
    Then the rest in Galilee :
    Then a cloud in glory bore
    Thee to Thine own native shore.

B   oldly David pour'd the strain :
    GOD ascends to Heav'n again :
    With the trumpet's pealing note
    Alleluias round Him float ;
    As He now, by hard-won right,
    Seeks the Fount of purest Light !

C rime on crime, and grief on grief,
    Left the world without relief:
    Now that aged, languid race,
    GOD hath quickened by His grace :
    As Thy going up we see,
    Glory to Thy Glory be !

Catavasía.

θέιῳ καλυφθείς.

D arkness and awe, when Sinai's top he
    trod,
    Taught him of faltering tongue the Law
    of GOD.
    The mist was scattered from his spirit's
    eye,
    He prais'd and hymn'd the Maker of
    the sky,
When He That is and was and shall be,
    passed by.

ODE III.

ἐπάρατε πυλάς.

" E xalt, exalt, the Heavenly Gates,
　　Ye chiefs of mighty name!
　The Lord and King of all things waits,
　　Enrob'd in earthly frame:"
　So to the higher seats they cry,
　The humbler legions of the sky.

F 　or Adam, by the Serpent's guile,
　　Distress'd, deceiv'd, o'erthrown,
　Thou left'st Thy native Home awhile,
　　Thou left'st the FATHER'S Throne :
　Now he is deck'd afresh with grace,
　Thou seek'st once more the Heav'nly
　　place.

G 　lad festal keeps the earth to day,
　　Glad festal Heav'n is keeping :
　The Ascension-pomp, in bright array,
　　Goes proudly sky-ward sweeping :
　The LORD the mighty deed hath done,
　And join'd the severed into one.

Catavasía.

ἔρρηξε γαστρός.

H er fetters of the barren womb it rent,
　　It crush'd the malice of the insolent,
　　The cry of her—the prophetess, who
　　　　brought
　　A contrite spirit, and a humble thought
To Him, Who bids His Throne by earnest
　　　　prayer be sought.

ODE IV.

Ἰησοῦς ὁ ζωοδότης.

J esus, Lord of Life Eternal,
  Taking those He lov'd the best,
Stood upon the Mount of Olives,
  And His Own the last time blest:
Then, though He had never left it,
  Sought again His Father's breast.

K now, O world, this highest festal:
  Floods and oceans, clap your hands!
Angels, raise the song of triumph!
  Make response, ye distant lands!
For our flesh is knit to Godhead,
  Knit in everlasting bands!

L oosing Death with all its terrors
  Thou ascended'st up on high,
And to mortals, now Immortal,
  Gavest immortality:
As Thine own Disciples saw Thee
  Mounting victor to the sky!

L

Catavasia.

M onarch of monarchs, Sole of Sole, to
    Thee,
    WORD, glorious in Thy FATHER's
    Majesty,
    And sending Thy co-equal SPIRIT
    bright
    To teach, to comfort, and to guide
    aright,
Thine own Apostles sang : All glory to
    Thy might !

ODE V.

νεκρώσας τὸν θάνατον.

N   ow that Death by death hath found its
      ending,
      Thou dost call to Thee Thy lov'd
        Eleven;
    And from holy Olivet ascending
      On a cloud art carried up to Heaven.

O   that wondrous Birth! that wondrous
      Rising!
      That more wondrous mounting to
        the sky!
    So Elias, earthly things despising,
      In a fiery chariot went on high.

P   arted from Him, still they watch'd His
      going:
      'Why stand gazing thus?' the Angel
        said:
    'This same JESUS, all His glory showing,
      'Shall return to judge the quick and
        dead.'

Catavasia.

Q   uicken'd and cleans'd, receive remission
     new
     In the descending SPIRIT's fiery dew,
     Sons of the Church, and light-formed
       generation !
     For lo ! the law goes forth from Sion's
       nation,
     The cloven tongues of flame, the
       PARACLETE's salvation !

ODE VI.
ῥανάτωσαν ἡμῖν ἄνωθεν.

R   ain down, ye heav'ns, eternal bliss!
    The Cherub-cloud to-day
  Bears JESUS where His Father is,
    Along the starry way!

S   un der'd of old were Heav'n and Earth:
    But Thou, Incarnate King!
  Hast made them one by that Thy Birth,
    And this Thy triumphing.

' T   hy victor-raiment, wherefore red?
    What mean the marks of pain
  That print Thy form?'—the Angels said,
    The ascending Monarch's train.

Catavasía.

V   ery Oblation, by the scourges torn!
    Nailed to the bitter Cross, O Virgin-
      born!
  As once the Prophet from the monster's
    maw,
 So now Thy love, accomplishing the Law,
Adam from utter death to perfect Life
    would draw.

Oicos.

τὰ τῆς γῆς ἐπὶ τῆς γῆς.

Things of the earth in the earth will we lay,
Ashes with ashes, the dust with the clay :
Lift up the heart, and the eye, and the love,
Lift up thyself, to the regions above :
Since the Immortal hath entered of late,
Mortals may pass at the Heavenly gate.—
Stand we on Olivet : mark Him ascend,
Whose is the glory and might without end ;
There, with His own ones, the Giver of Good
Blessing them once more, a little while stood.
" Nothing can part us,—nor distance, nor
     foes ;—
Lo! I am for you, and who can oppose ?"

ODE VII.

φωτεινή σε, φῶς.

W afting Him up on high,
    The glorious cloud receives
The LORD of Immortality,
    And earth the Victor leaves:
The Heavenly People raise the strain,
The Apostles pour the hymn again ;—
    GOD of our Fathers, Thou art blest !

Y e faithful, tell your joys !
    All hearts with gladness bound !
GOD is gone up with a merry noise,—
    The LORD with the trumpet's sound !
To Him we cry, by woes once tried,
Now glorious at the FATHER's side,—
    GOD of our Fathers, Thou art blest !

Z   ealous for GOD of yore,
   With zeal still Moses burns :
  " Come, Heavenly Spirits, and adore
   The Victor Who returns :
  Rise, Angel legions, rise and sing
  The ancient hymn to greet the King,
   GOD of our Fathers, Thou art blest!"

Catavasía.

J   oin'd with the trumpet-peal, the din
   and shout,
  Cornet, flute, sackbut, dulcimer rang
   out,
  And bade adore the golden Deity :
  The SPIRIT's gentler voice gives praise
   to Thee,
O co-eternal One—O consubstantial Three !

ODE VIII. (1)

Hirmos. HIM OF THE FATHER.

τὸν ἐν δυσὶ ταῖς οὐσίαις.

O   f twofold natures, CHRIST, the Giver
  Of immortality and love,
  Ascendeth to the FATHER's glory,
   Ascendeth to the Throne above :
    Wherefore He, this glorious morn,
     Be by all ador'd´:
    Thou That liftest up our horn,
     Holy art Thou, LORD !

S   laves are set free, and captives ransom'd :
  The Nature that He made at first
  He now presenteth to the FATHER,
   The chains of her damnation burst :
    This the cause that He was born,
     Adam's race restor'd :
    Thou That liftest up our horn,
     Holy art Thou, LORD !

E   mptied awhile of all His brightness,
        He enter'd thus the glorious fight;
    O'erthrew the foe, mankind exalted
        Far above every Pow'r and Might:
            Therefore bare He pains and scorn,
                Calvary's heart-blood pour'd:—
            Thou That liftest up our horn,
                Holy art Thou, LORD!

Catavasía.

P   raising the LORD they stood, the
        Martyr Three,
    Untouch'd amidst the fire, and wholly
        free:
    With them associate, let the world's
        wide frame
    To Him Whose healing dew restrain'd
        the flame,
    Send up the hymn of praise, and magnify
        His Name!

(1) I have specified this Hirmos, because the
reader can see it by turning back to page 71.

ODE IX.

ὦ τῶν δωρεῶν.

H   oly gift, surpassing comprehension !
Wond'rous mystery of each fiery tongue !
CHRIST made good His Promise in
    Ascension :
O'er the Twelve the cloven flames have
    hung !

S   pake the LORD, or ere He left the
    Eleven :
"Here in Salem wait the Gift I send :
Till the PARACLETE came down from
    Heav'n,
Everlasting Guide and Guard and
    Friend."

O   that shame, now ended in His glory !
O that pain, now lost in joy unknown !
Tell it out with praise, the whole glad
    story,
Human nature at the FATHER's throne !

Catavasia.

D   eclare, ye Angel Bands that dwell on
     high,
     How saw ye Him, the Victor, drawing
      nigh?
     What strange new visions burst upon
      your sight?
     One in the Form of Man, That claims
      by right
   The very throne of GOD, the unapproached
     Light!

Exaposteilarion.

E   ternal!   After Thine own will
     Thou born in time would'st be:
   After the self-same counsel still
     Was Thine Epiphany:
   Thou in our flesh didst yield Thy breath,
     Immortal GOD, for man:
   Thou by Thy death didst conquer Death,
     Through Thine Almighty plan.
   Thou, rising Victor to the sky,
     Fill'st Heav'n and earth above:
   And send'st the Promise from on high,
     The SPIRIT of Thy Love!

Theoctistus of the Studium.

+ *Circ.* A.D. 890.

He is said to have been the friend of S. Joseph; but is only known to us by the "Suppliant Canon to JESUS," to be found at the end of the *Paracletice.* The following is a Cento formed from it.

'Ιησοῦ γλυκύτατε.

JESU, Name all names above,
　JESU, best and dearest,
JESU, Fount of perfect love,
　Holiest, tenderest, nearest;
JESU, source of grace completest,
JESU purest, JESU sweetest,
　JESU, Well of power Divine,
　Make me, keep me, seal me Thine!

JESU, open me the gate
   That of old he enter'd,
Who, in that most lost estate,
   Wholly on Thee ventur'd;
Thou, Whose Wounds are ever pleading,
And Thy Passion interceding,
   From my misery let me rise
   To a Home in Paradise !

Thou didst call the Prodigal :
   Thou didst pardon Mary :
Thou Whose words can never fall,
   Love can never vary :
LORD, amidst my lost condition
Give—for Thou can'st give—contrition!
   Thou can'st pardon all mine ill
   If Thou wilt : O say, " I will !"

Woe, that I have turned aside
   After fleshly pleasure !
Woe, that I have never tried
   For the Heavenly Treasure !
Treasure, safe in Homes supernal ;
Incorruptible, eternal !
   Treasure no less price hath won
   Than the Passion of The SON !

Jesu, crown'd with Thorns for me!
 Scourged for my transgression!
Witnessing, through agony,
 That Thy good confession;
Jesu, clad in purple raiment,
For my evils making payment;
 Let not all Thy woe and pain,
 Let not Calvary, be in vain!

When I reach Death's bitter sea
 And its waves roll higher,
Help the more forsaking me
 As the storm draws nigher:
Jesu, leave me not to languish,
Helpless, hopeless, full of anguish!
 Tell me,—Verily I say,
 Thou shall be with Me to-day!

Metrophanes of Smyrna.

✝ *Circ.* A.D. 910.

He was Bishop of that See towards the
close of the 9th century, and is principally
famous for his Canons in honour of the
Blessed TRINITY,—eight in number, one to
each Tone. They are sung at Matins on
Sundays : and if the writer has not always
been able to fuse his learning and orthodoxy
into poetry, nor yet to escape the tautology
of his brother bards, these compositions are
stately and striking. Metrophanes was a
vigorous supporter of S. Ignatius ; and the
partisan of Rome in her contest with
Photius.

It would be impossible, without wearying
the reader, to translate the whole of one
of the Triadic Canons ; but a Cento from
them may not be unacceptable.

O UNITY OF THREEFOLD LIGHT.

τριφεγγὴς Μονὰς θεαρχική.

[From the Canon for Sunday of the Second Tone.]

O Unity of Threefold Light,
   Send out Thy loveliest ray,
And scatter our transgressions' night,
   And turn it into day!
Make us those temples, pure and fair,
   Thy glory loveth well,
The spotless tabernacles, where
   Thou may'st vouchsafe to dwell!

The glorious hosts of peerless might
   That ever see Thy Face,
Thou mak'st the mirrors of Thy Light,
   The vessels of Thy grace:
Thou, when their wond'rous strain they
      weave,
   Hast pleasure in the lay:
Deign thus our praises to receive,
   Albeit from lips of clay!

M

And yet Thyself they cannot know,
  Nor pierce the veil of light
That hides Thee from the Thrones below,
  As in profoundest night :
How then can mortal accents frame
  Due tribute to their King ?
Thou, only, while we praise Thy Name,
  Forgive us as we sing !

~~~~~~~~

Beyond Metrophanes, it will not be necessary to carry our translations. The following names may, however, be mentioned.

Euthymius.

✝ A.D. 910.

Euthymius, usually known as Syngelus, (the same as *Syncellus*, the confidential Deacon of the Patriarch of Constantinople,) who died about 916, is the author of a Penitential Canon to S. Mary, which is highly esteemed in the East. It would scarcely, however, be possible to make even a Cento from it, which should be acceptable to the English reader.

Leo VI.

✝ A.D. 917.

Our next name is that of a Royal Poet. Leo VI., the Philosopher, who reigned from 886 to 917, left behind him the *Idiomela*, or detached stanzas, on the Resurrection, sung at Lauds. They are better than might have been expected from an Imperial author, and the troubler of the Eastern Church by a *fourth* marriage.

The same thing may be said of the Exaposteilaria of his son, Constantine Porphyrogenitus, whose life lasted till 959.

John Mauropus.

+ A.D. 1060.

John Mauropus, Metropolitan of Euchaïta, sometimes called the last of the Greek Fathers, left a number of hymns, printed at Eton in 1610 : and if not boasting much poetical fire, at least graced with a gentle and Isocratean eloquence. As they have not been employed by the Church, they claim no further notice here.

With this Metropolitan, Greek Hymnology well-nigh ceased : at least the only other name that need be mentioned is that of Philotheus, Patriarch of Constantinople, who died in 1376. This man, the warm supporter of the dogma of the *Uncreated Light*, was the composer of several stanzas for Orthodoxy Sunday, and the Canon for July 16, on the Holy Fathers: both in the very worst taste.

J. T. HAYES, Lyall Place, Eaton Square.